Buddy Helms has written a fascinating, double-braided circle of a book about marriage. Or is it a detailed double-helix of a book about the church? Actually, it's both. Helms explores the Bible's teachings about marriage as well as its metaphors that compare "the Bride of Christ" to marriage. Studying both marriage and church, he offers a layered, nuanced interpretation of Scripture that simultaneously will strengthen marriages and intensify Christians' understanding of the intimate relationship between Christ and His church.

—Marv Knox, Editor of the *Baptist Standard*

In a day when many believers doubt that Christian marriage ideals can be lived out in modern times, Helms has delivered a very thought-provoking work that gives hope to the believer that God's design for marriage can be lived out victoriously.

—Dave T. Gentry, PhD.,
Founding Director, Westwood Ministries

Buddy Helms has accomplished something quite remarkable. He has tackled a difficult, controversial subject, handled it with both grace and scholarship, and then presented his convictions in an easy-to-read, engaging style. The moments spent with this book will cause the reader to celebrate God's love and equip the reader to share that love with others.

—Dr. Richard Jackson, Pastor Emeritus,
North Phoenix Baptist Church, and
President, Jackson Center for Evangelism
& Encouragement, Brownwood, TX

MARRIAGE

WHAT'S THE
BIG DEAL?

BUDDY HELMS

MARRIAGE
WHAT'S THE BIG DEAL?

Tate Publishing & Enterprises

Published by Tate Publishing & Enterprises, LLC
127 E. Trade Center Terrace | Mustang, Oklahoma 73064 USA
1.888.361.9473 | www.tatepublishing.com

Tate Publishing is committed to excellence in the publishing industry. The company reflects the philosophy established by the founders, based on Psalm 68:11,
"The Lord gave the word and great was the company of those who published it."

Book design copyright © 2010 by Tate Publishing, LLC. All rights reserved.
Cover design by Kellie Southerland
Interior design by Joey Garrett

Published in the United States of America

ISBN: 978-1-61663-161-1
1. Religion / Christian Life / Love & Marriag
2. Religion / Biblical Studies / History & Culture
10.03.15

DEDICATION

This book is dedicated first to the Lord Jesus Christ, who has given me life and who continues to teach me about relationships; and secondly, to my wife, Carla, whom Christ has blessed with a truly loving and giving spirit, and whom he has used to teach me more and more every day.

ACKNOWLEDGMENTS

I would like to thank God, first, for the inspiration and the ability to put this together for his glory. Before beginning any research, God placed this subject on my heart, and the research has been eye-opening.

I would also like to thank the staff of the Reagan County Library for tracking down all the books that I needed to complete the research.

Although I have never met him in person, I would also like to thank Gary Thomas, whose book, *Sacred Marriage,* is inspiring and informative, and I highly recommend that every couple read it.

All biblical quotes that I use in this book are from the King James Version. There are a few exceptions within quotes from other authors, but they are noted in the text.

TABLE OF CONTENTS

FOREWORD

It is with a great deal of appreciation that I peruse this
new work by Buddy Helms entitled *Marriage: What's
the Deal?* In a day when the cultural church has bought
in so much of each modern culture's view of marriage,
it is refreshing to read a biblically centered work that
holds marriage up to God's original intent. As you read
this book, it may well become a resource for you to
use in your own marriage, future marriage, or in helping others in their marriage journey. Buddy has done
a good work in bringing the Scripture to bear on the
modern's life. As the author weaves the challenges that
modern man experiences in marriage with the Bible's
directives and design for marriage, the book emerges
as a very practical biblical resource for doing marriage
in any age and in any culture. In a day when many
believers doubt that Christian marriage ideals can
be lived out in modern times, Helms has delivered a
very thought-provoking work that gives hope to the
believer that God's design for marriage can be lived out
victoriously.

I have known Buddy Helms and his family for many years. What you see on the pages of this book has been proven in the laboratory of life by the author and his family. They have truly lived out the role of over comer. I have watched them persevere in marriage and family and do so in the "fish bowl" of ministry. Buddy has pastored successfully over the years and has managed to prioritize marriage and family even in the midst of ministry. What you will read in the pages of this book has indeed been fleshed out in the life of the author. As with many of us, the author has lived and learned by applying God's principles and by the victories and failures in his own life. We reap the benefit of the life lessons learned by this author, who has remained steadfast for God down through the years. He writes regarding God's directives and principles with the knowledge that they are true and that God does exactly what he promises.

Most of all I count Buddy Helms as a friend. Anyone who knows how to do friendship has a good handle on how to do marriage. As you read these pages, read with the confidence that God is using a man of faith to communicate Father's truths to a spiritually hungry world. Many will read this work and their lives will be changed. I pray that you as a reader will be one of those fortunate people.

—Dave T. Gentry, PhD.
Founding Director
Westwood Ministries

INTRODUCTION

We seem to hear something about marriage or marital rights almost daily. Marriage has been an issue for years, and it has been cussed and discussed, joked about, and even blatantly mocked. There seems to be some misunderstanding about marriage and what it is all about. The government regulates it and has historically decided who can and can't get married, and the argument continues. This book is not about governmental regulation of marriage. This book will approach the subject from its inception. When did marriage begin, and who invented it? Marriage will be examined from a biblical perspective. As a theologian, I have a biblical worldview, and I would like to examine some of the biblical reasons for marriage. We will even talk a little bit about divorce. Why is marriage important? Why do so many oppose the idea of gay marriage? What's the deal? Why do some marry, divorce, and then remarry over and over like they change their socks? There seems to be a great deal of confusion about the origin of marriage, the purpose of marriage, and the importance of marriage. Have you ever wondered what God thinks of this whole marriage and divorce mess? God invented marriage as a blessing and a revelation, but he allowed divorce because of sin and the hardness of men's hearts.

In premarital counseling, we talk about many things, but I always ask every prospective bride and groom the same question at some point during the first interview. Why do you want to get married? Invariably, they will say that they are in love. Is being in love enough? Do they even understand what that means? Some tell me that they believe that God has brought them together, but even for this group, the marriage isn't bulletproof. What does the Bible say? What is God trying to teach us in marriage? Should we be more concerned with the rites or the rights of marriage? *Rites* are a particular form or manner governing the words or actions for a ceremony. It refers to the ceremonial practices of a church or group of churches or a ceremonial act. Perhaps we should be more interested in God's purposes and plans for marriage than we are about our rights or the rites of marriage. The ceremony doesn't last very long, but the commitment is for a lifetime. At least it should be. This book will look at messages from God that are hidden in plain sight in the Bible about marriage. But are they really hidden, or have they simply been ignored or overlooked?

There has been much written about Bible codes, but for the most part, they seem to focus on what will happen in the future. What about right now? What does God want us to be doing at this moment? What does he want us to understand? What does he want us to learn and apply in our lives today? What is God trying to tell us? Why aren't we listening? In order to find these Bible codes that are hidden in the Old Testament, a computer is required with the proper programming to search though the Hebrew text for equally spaced letters that the researchers say represent times, places, names, and specific events that will take place in the future, but most of what they turn up is discovered after the fact. We hear of fulfilled prophecy hidden within the writings of Nostradamus, and volumes are written about his quatrains, which are a unit or group of four lines of verse, and the predictions that may be discovered in them. But what good is prophecy if it is only discovered after the event has occurred, and why are people so fascinated by the future?

This book will not focus on prophecy of future events but will examine God's code in the Bible with its hidden messages that have been a mystery for far too long. In a sense, it is about the future, yours and mine. Our future depends on the decisions that we make today! Don't you just hate it when solutions and answers seem to elude your grasp? I have heard people say that the best place to hide something is in plain sight, and this is exactly where these mysteries are hidden. They are in plain sight of anyone who might choose to read and discover them through the leadership of the Holy Spirit. God has revelations for his people in Old Testament stories of factual history, in the Law of Moses, and in metaphors of his relationship to Israel. These hidden revelations are about how God wants us to live and act toward him and toward one another today, not in the future. Simple logic tells me that what God wants me to do today is much more important to my life and the lives of people living today than something he is planning to do a hundred or more years from now. Don't misunderstand. I believe that Christ could return for his church at any moment, but so did John, Paul, and Peter. In the meantime, what does God want us to be doing? What has he told us?

There are themes in Scripture that God has given us to reveal his plan for the welfare of humanity and to prepare us for eternity with him. New life, forgiveness, and deliverance from the sin in a person's life are received by grace through faith in the Lord Jesus Christ and in the power of his resurrection, but after a person receives Christ as Lord and Savior, God has a plan for his or her life. Ephesians 2:10 says, "For we are his workmanship, created in Christ Jesus unto good works, which God hath before ordained that we should walk in them." If God has "before ordained" that we should walk in good works, what are the works that he wants us to do, and how do we know if we are actually walking in those good works? The Bible has the answers, but many of the answers have been overlooked or completely missed, as many theologians dissect words and phrases rather than looking for God's complete meaning and revelation.

Isn't the Bible simple enough that anyone can understand its meaning? I have heard people say that anyone can understand the message of the Bible, and more and more modern translations have been produced to make it more understandable and easily readable. But if anyone can understand it, why do we need simpler versions? The truth is that the only way anyone can understand the meaning of God's Word is through the leadership and enlightenment of the Holy Spirit. God, the Holy Spirit, must open the eyes of the believer to receive his truth, and any believer in the atoning work of Christ Jesus should be able to understand God's Word. Perhaps this is why we have so many heretical views of Scripture and why so many discount and attempt to explain away the miraculous and the profound. Many theologians have a great deal of knowledge about the Bible, but it is more in their heads than in their hearts. Paul wrote to the church at Corinth:

> But we speak the wisdom of God in a mystery, even the hidden wisdom, which God ordained before the world unto our glory: Which none of the princes of this world knew: for had they known it, they would not have crucified the Lord of Glory. But as it is written, Eye hath not seen, nor ear heard, neither have entered into the heart of man, the things which God hath prepared for them that love him. But God hath revealed them unto us by his Spirit: for the Spirit searcheth all things, yea, the deep things of God. For what man knoweth the things of man, save the spirit of man which is in him? Even so the things of God knoweth no man, but the Spirit of God. Now we have received, not the spirit of the world, but the spirit which is of God; that we might know the things that are freely given to us of God.
>
> I Corinthians 2:7–12

Does wisdom have to be hidden from those who have a personal relationship with the Lord Jesus Christ?

According to the Apostle Paul, God has revealed them to us by his Spirit. What mysteries have you discovered? Are the things God has prepared for us only in heaven? Perhaps he has blessings that he wants us to receive right now, and perhaps there are people whom he wants us to bless just as he has blessed us. Many claim to desire knowledge of God's will for their lives, but if he reveals it, will they strive to do what he asks? God knows who will and who won't. He has a purpose for your life, but when you discover it, are you truly willing to do whatever he says and go wherever he sends? In that sense, this may be a dangerous study. We are responsible to God for the revelation we receive. Jesus said: "For unto whomsoever much is given, of him shall be much required: and to whom men have committed much, of him they will ask the more" (Luke 12:48b).

Most of the Bible was meant to be taken literally, but at times "word pictures" are used to illuminate God's meaning, and at times, things that are meant literally and should be taken literally have deeper meaning attached to them. Why do you suppose Paul wrote to Timothy about rightly dividing the word of truth? Consider the types that are found in the Old Testament that point to and reveal the meaning of things in the New Testament. Consider the parables of Christ and the metaphorical meaning of names and events. The very names of God are descriptive and revelatory. Come on along for the ride! Prepare to see, hear, and understand things that you may have read before in which you may have missed God's meaning. It has been hidden in plain sight.

METAPHORS OF LIFE

If you were trying to explain how to do something that someone had never done or even heard of before, how would you go about doing it? It would be much simpler if there were something they knew and understood with which you could compare the process. It would also be very helpful if you spoke their language. What if you were trying to explain a perfect relationship to people who had never really seen one before? Have you ever seen a perfect relationship? God first familiarized us with the concept of marriage in the Garden of Eden. God then uses marriage as a common comparative idea for the relationship that he desires to have with Israel and ultimately with the church. The Bible begins with a picture of marriage as we see Adam and Eve in the garden. God is trying to help us to understand by using the oldest and what should be one of the most commonly understood relationships known to humanity. It is supposed to be a covenant relationship between a man and a woman that lasts for a lifetime. But the world's attempt to cheapen and weaken man's understanding of the traditional and God-ordained marriage relationship seems to be an attempt to subvert the message of the Bible and limit man's understanding. The theological explanations surrounding marriage in the Scriptures are sometimes less than complete. God relates to us through covenant, and marriage should be approached as a covenant agreement in the presence of God, which should illustrate the relationship that God desires to have with his people.

God divorces Israel in Jeremiah 3:6–23 because of their backsliding and harlotry and warns Judah with this example. Verse 8 says that God gave her, Israel, a "bill of divorce," and if this is to be taken literally, every Israelite should have received a copy. In a sense, they did receive a written decree from God through the prophet Jeremiah. So that the prophet Hosea will have a better understanding of God's struggle to have a lasting relationship with Israel through a covenant relationship, God tells him to marry a whore in Hosea 1:2. This can also be seen as a sign and a reminder to Israel that God expects them to be faithful like a virtuous wife, unlike Gomer.

One of the most forgotten and misunderstood lines in the marriage ceremony seems to be "forsaking all others." If the two are to become "one," forsaking *all* others may also refer to forsaking one's self. Marriages fail many times because one or both partners begin to think: *It's all about me and my needs.* Obviously, when a relationship with God fails, it is never God's fault, for God is love, and he cannot lie or sin, and he has promised to never leave nor forsake us. On the other hand, his people have continually left and forsaken him.

The marriage relationship metaphor is continued in the New Testament with the church being called the bride of Christ. But something has changed. The success of the marriage no longer depends upon the bride's ability to keep the vows (commandments) but rests solely upon the redemptive work of the risen Lord. This does not mean that the vows are not important but that the new relationship all hinges upon God's grace. Marriage should not be about following a set of rules and regulations. If a couple simply moves in together and starts acting as if they are married, we used to say that they were "living in sin." If they split up, there would be no vows broken because they didn't say any. No divorce is needed because they weren't ever really married; however, common law can come into the picture. With God, there are no common law marriages. If a person never commits to a belief and trust in Christ but merely decides to clean up their life, start going to church, and live by the Ten Commandments, they have no personal relationship with God. They are living in sin. They are still separated from God, and they are self righteous, not possessing the righteousness of Christ. Marriage should be about loving one another unconditionally as God loves us, and it should be a true spiritual union that is blessed by God and centered in the couple's relationship with God in Christ Jesus and with one another. But can a human love as God loves and make this kind of holy union work? The answer to this question is *yes!* But it takes the miracle of God's grace.

Men and women must become new creations in Christ Jesus, and they must understand that the quality of the relationship depends upon God's grace together with the human commitment to his will and to the marriage. We may create a parody of James 2:18 and relate it to marriage by saying: "Show me your love without working at it, and I will show you my love by working to improve and enhance our marriage relationship." Remember that what I am describing here is God's perfect plan for revelation and for the welfare of humanity. Can non-Christians have a long and happy relationship within the bonds of matrimony? Of course they can, but if God is left out of the equation, there is no witness to God's plan for spiritual union with a redeemed people according to his will. Instead, the couple are "thumbing their noses" at God and saying to him, their friends, their families, and to the world that they don't need the God of the Bible or the shed blood of Christ.

I realize that some of my fundamentalist friends will think I am a heretic for saying this, but God did not intend for us to take everything in the Bible literally. They will ask me how to decide to take something literally or not. Simply stated, when God says to do something or don't do something, we had better take it literally, but here are some examples of some verses that we should take seriously but not literally. In Exodus 19:4, God did not literally send a giant eagle to carry Israel out of Egypt. He was using a metaphor to explain that their deliverance was supernatural and to remind them that it was by his power that they were set free. Also, "they that wait upon the Lord," in Isaiah 40:31 are not really going to sprout eagles' wings and fly away. "They shall mount up on wings as eagles," in

Isaiah, is a simile. Any time that Jesus starts a parable with "The kingdom of heaven is like ... ," he is about to deliver another simile. He does this several times in the gospel of Matthew. It is simply a fact that God uses figures of speech in the Bible. In Genesis 49:4, it says: "Judah is a lion's whelp [metaphor]: from the prey, my son, thou art gone up: he stooped down, he couched as a lion [simile], and as an old lion [simile]; who shall rouse him up?" Here is a metaphor followed by two similes in the same verse. Jacob said this as he was prophesying over or blessing his sons. He also said that Naphtali is a "hind let loose" (metaphor), and Joseph is a "fruitful bough" (metaphor) in Genesis 49:21–22. Deuteronomy 32:4 says that "God is the Rock" (metaphor). What about the word picture used to describe Christ as the Lion of the tribe of Judah and the root of David in Revelation 5:5? Does this mean that we are to picture Jesus as a big furry cat with a long mane and a tail or a tree root coming out of the ground? No! So, when the church is called the bride of Christ, does this mean that we are all going to be somehow melded together to form one woman in a white dress, and we need to start looking for something old, new, borrowed, and blue? No, again! But it does mean that God expects us to be one with Christ, and he wants us to be "one brotherhood united in fellowship and in love," just as the pledge to the Christian flag states. It means that he desires an intimate relationship with us that involves love, trust, and commitment. He wants to maintain communication and take part in every aspect of our lives, giving, caring, and sharing in every part of our existence. The church is the bride of Christ, and we are supposed to be one flesh with him, but in Christ, as it should be in a Christian marriage, the relationship goes beyond the mere flesh and extends to the spirit. It is no accident that the church is also referred to as the body of Christ. Christians are supposed to be one with Christ. They are supposed to have the mind of Christ, and they are supposed to be dead to self and alive to God.

God uses figures of speech so that we can better understand his love for us. He wants to give us insights into the relationship that he desires to have with us, and he wants to give us spiritual insights through the use of these types, metaphors, and similes. We should be wary of all-inclusive statements about the Bible like: "Every word of the Bible is to be taken literally. It is all God's Word." Is it God's Word when the devil or a demoniac is speaking? Is it God's Word when the Pharisees accuse Jesus of having a demon or casting out demons by the power of Beelzebub? No. But it is God's record of these things happening. God records the mistakes of people in the Bible, and he expects us to learn from their mistakes so that we don't repeat them. When the Pharisees brought the woman caught in the act of adultery to Jesus, they were acting cold and heartless, and they were breaking the law. Where was the man in this situation? They were not really concerned about justice or the law. They were simply looking for an opportunity to trap and accuse Jesus in whatever answer he might give.

It has been said that a parable is an earthly story with a heavenly meaning. I would like to explore the heavenly meaning that may be found in God's use of the metaphors of marriage, divorce, building, foundation, and the potter's wheel. I believe that God has reasons for everything that he says and does. We must remember, however, as we study metaphors, that they are word pictures, and though they are not always realities, the message is real, and ignoring any message from God has catastrophic consequences. Seeking to enforce the law apart from the love of God has driven more people away from God than we can imagine. Why does the church, which is saved by grace, continually seek to return to legalism and dictate to the world how they should live? I think that it is more about a desire to be in control than it is an effort to seek righteousness. It is a modern-day Pharisaic mind-set. How's your heart? What is your primary focus? Is it God and his love and love for others, or is it legality? Paul warned the church in Galatians 5:4, "Christ is become of no effect unto you, whosoever of you are justified by the law; ye are fallen from grace." Remember that Jesus touched the leper, ate with tax collectors and sinners, spoke openly with the woman at the well, called uneducated fishermen to be disciples, said that the Sabbath was made for man, not man for the Sabbath, and to the woman taken in the very act of adultery, he said, "Neither do I condemn thee: go, and sin no more" (John 8:11b). Many today who claim to be Christians would be more likely to want to cast the first stone. The Lord Jesus Christ was obviously on a specific mission, and he delivered the message of the Father in the love of the Father in obedience to the will of the Father, but the message was not the ultimate purpose of his mission. He came to offer himself as a sacrifice for sins. In John 12:49,

Jesus says: "For I have not spoken of myself; but the Father which sent me, he gave me a commandment, what I should say, and what I should speak."

A perfect example of literal thinking that prevented communication may be seen in the third chapter of the Gospel of John. Nicodemus did not understand how a grown man could be born again. Jesus' words involved a spiritual birth, not a physical birth. Later in John 6:51–56, Jesus did not expect his followers to actually eat his flesh and drink his blood. He was speaking figuratively about something that would become clear after his resurrection. When God speaks, we should listen very closely, not just to the words but to his message. Sometimes, it is hidden in a historical story, a symbol, a type, a parable, a simile, or even a metaphor.

I do not think that it was an accident or a coincidence that Christ began his wondrous works at the *marriage* at Cana of Galilee *on the third day* in John 2:1. We are all looking forward, at least those of us who trust in Christ, to the marriage supper of the Lamb. Was it simply an accident that the first miracle was done at a wedding feast? I don't think so. Too many times, we read the words of Scripture and jump immediately to the conclusion that what we see on the surface is exactly what God wants us to learn, nothing more and nothing less. How big is your God? I also do not think that it was a coincidence that the water that was drawn out of those pots that became wine had been set aside for ceremonial cleansing, especially when we consider the meaning of the wine used in the Lord's Supper. Many argue loudly that the Bible is the complete, inerrant Word of God, but when presented with a deeper meaning, they shy away for fear of being caught up in a cult or of being deceived by false teaching. When we use the word *inerrant*, do people understand what we mean, and do we fully understand it ourselves? This is a mighty big word for a people whose leaders don't always understand the meaning of the word *is*. I believe that God started trying to reveal his perfect will to us in Genesis 1:1, and he was not finished until Revelation 22:21. It is the complete truth without any mixture of error. It was literally God-breathed. But God did not just give us a book. He gave us his own indwelling spirit to guide us and help us to understand that book that was written by men who were also guided by his Spirit as they recorded every word that he wanted us to receive.

As I have already stated, I believe that everything that God tells us is for a purpose, and many times, he has purposes that go beyond the obvious. God instituted marriage for the welfare of humanity, to fill the earth, to provide blessings untold, and perhaps even to reveal something much greater to humanity, but the devil wants to destroy all of God's perfect gifts and hide the truth from those who would diligently seek it. It seems to be no accident or coincidence that God begins the book of Genesis with the marriage of Adam and Eve and ends the book of Revelation with the marriage of the Lamb. "And the spirit and the bride say, Come. And let him that heareth say, Come. And let him that is athirst come. And whosoever will, let him take the water of life freely" (Revelation 22:17). So, if you have spiritual ears to hear, then listen closely.

Let's consider a prophecy of Jesus Christ concerning his Second Coming.

> But as the days of Noe were, so shall the coming of the Son of man be. For as in the days that were before the flood they were eating and drinking, marrying and giving in marriage, until the day that Noe entered into the ark, And knew not until the flood came, and took them all away; so shall also the coming of the Son of man be.
>
> Matthew 24:37–39

It would be easy to quickly pass over this prophecy and say that Jesus is only referring to the fact that people were just going about their everyday routines before the flood, and they will be doing the same when Jesus returns, and they will be completely surprised at his return. If we review several commentaries, we will find that this is the general consensus, but as we come to the conclusion of this book, I hope that we may look at it differently, especially since Christ mentions marriage in this prophecy. It is ironic that they will routinely be doing something that should reveal God's plan to have a personal relationship with them, but they will not understand.

How important is God's use of metaphor in the Bible? If God is trying to reveal truth to his people, how significant do you think that effort is to him or to us? We use metaphors constantly in everyday language, and Jesus used them to illustrate and explain the points that he was making to his disciples. The trail of the metaphor of marriage and divorce in the Bible is simply too big to ignore. I love biblical exegesis, but it is possible to spend so much time and effort dissecting Greek and Hebrew words that one completely misses the big picture that God is trying to paint. God, unlike humanity, does not do anything haphazardly. When we see an obvious theme in the Bible that is consistent from cover to cover, it should become clear that God has a message that he wants his people to understand. This may be accomplished with the help of the Holy Spirit and some diligent study along with sound methods of biblical interpretation. A little common sense is also required. Many are afraid to attempt this journey into God's use of metaphor. I think that it is because people have a tendency to fear what they do not understand or what they perceive others will not fully understand. To avoid confusion, should we remove all the miracles from the Bible, like Thomas Jefferson, and then also remove all the metaphors and similes? No. I believe the Bible is the complete revelation of God and his plan for our salvation, and to ignore any of that Word would be a colossal mistake.

God uses metaphor to reveal himself, and he also uses it to reveal what he expects of us. The metaphor of marriage reveals God as one who loves us more than life itself since he gave himself for us, while revealing to his children the relationship he desires to have with them in numerous ways. Did Jesus use metaphor? Consider the parables and the following statements from the Gospel of John. Jesus said:

I am the bread of life.

John 6:35

I am the bread which came down from heaven.

John 6:41

I am the living bread.

John 6:51

I am the light of the world.

John 9:5

I am the door of the sheep.

John 10:7

I am the good shepherd.

John 10:11, 14

I am the resurrection and the life.

John 11:25

I am the way, the truth, and the Life.

John 14:6

I am the true vine, and my Father is the husbandman.

John 15:1

All these are metaphors that reveal who Christ is. God reveals himself through metaphor, and he reveals who he wants us to become. He wants us to become loving members of his family who are sealed by his spirit, and we should be growing in Christ. Should we remove all the metaphors or simply ignore them?

Remember that it is a huge mistake to ignore anything that God has said, and editing out parts of the Bible that we may not like or fully understand should never be considered as an option.

Genesis is a book of beginnings, and we see the crowning glory of God's creation completed as he places Adam and Eve in the Garden and blesses them: "And God saw everything that he had made, and, behold, it was very good. And the evening and the morning were the sixth day" (Genesis 1:31). In chapter two, God reiterates and explains a little more of the creation process and reveals the need for Adam to have companionship and a suitable helper, which is to be fulfilled in Eve. The closing words of this chapter should sound very familiar to many people because they may have heard at least some of them at a wedding. Speaking of Eve, Adam says:

> This is now bone of my bones, and flesh of my flesh: she shall be called Woman, because she was taken out of Man. Therefore shall a man leave his father and mother, and shall cleave unto his wife: and they shall be one flesh. And they were both naked, the man and his wife, and were not ashamed.
>
> Genesis 2:23–25

In reading Genesis, have you ever considered Adam to be the first prophet of God? How could Adam have spoken of a man leaving his father and mother when he did not have parents? God had created him from the dust of the ground. He had to be speaking of his own descendants, and that would make this a prophecy. Not only is it a prophecy, but Jesus would later quote what Adam said about marriage in Mark 10:7. Also, did God really need to tell Adam and Eve to be fruitful and multiply and fill the earth in Genesis 1:28, or could he possibly have had another reason for this statement? Well, obviously sex was not the forbidden fruit, because God told them to have lots of it. But if we pair this with a New Testament verse like John 15:8, we hear Jesus say: "Herein is my Father glorified, that ye bear much fruit; so shall ye be my disciples." Do you think there is a parallel here, or am I just imagining it? This is what Christ expects of his bride. He wants us to grow up and bear fruit, but we can't do it without him. Okay, come back to earth.

In receiving Christ as Lord and Savior, one must leave all behind and cleave to the Lord, trusting him completely. Scripturally, we are to die to self and become new creations in Christ while becoming one with the Lord as we become a part of his bride and his body. So, a man must leave his father and mother, being joined to his wife to become one flesh, and a relationship with Christ requires death to an old way of life as a believer becomes one with Christ and is identified as part of the body of Christ and the bride of Christ. Is there a parallel here? Of course there is. What Adam said relates to what Christ did to redeem his people by shedding his blood, and all who will accept his salvation and the applied blood that purifies and sets us free from the fall must forsake all to follow Christ as they trust in him and him alone for salvation and life. But there is a lot of resistance to this call to die to self. We live in an *it's all about me* generation, and it seems to be getting worse by the minute.

God, in his book of beginnings, began with a marriage. Why was everything considered good up to this point, but when God completed his creative work with Adam and Eve he described it as very good? What is the significance of this creative act? From the very beginning, God began to demonstrate the need for companionship and love. Why do you suppose that one of the worst punishments that prisoners have endured over the centuries is solitary confinement? God created us with a need for one another and gave us a desire to interact with one another. God desires an intimate relationship with all of his creation, but sin has raised a wall of separation that prevents communication, and a separation of humanity from God is a much bigger problem than separation of church and state. The companionship and love that is most important is a relationship with God who is spirit in nature and invisible to human eyes. He is everywhere, but we cannot see him. Man needed a visible and physical manifestation that he could relate to, and God created woman. The Bible says: "So God created man in his own image, in the image of God created he him; male and female created he them" (Genesis 1:27). They couldn't see God, but when they looked at each other, they could see a reflection of his image. But did they really see God in each other? Adam saw a woman, and Eve saw a man, but with the revelation we have received, we should see much more. God wanted us to have companionship within a covenant relationship with our spouses to teach us of the relationship that he desires to have with us.

I believe that this whole story about Adam and Eve is absolutely true, and I believe it happened in exactly this way. I believe that God created the world in six literal 24-hour days. You can choose to believe whatever you like, but I believe the Bible. What are we to learn from the Genesis account of creation? This is not a metaphor in the sense that it is merely a story with a revelatory meaning. It is history, but let's examine how metaphor seems to be involved. Bernard Ramm wrote: "A metaphor expresses something by direct comparison, direct similarity, or direct parallelism."[1] When we consider the totality of biblical revelation and take into account the many times that marriage is mentioned, we must ask ourselves what meanings are attached to this beginning of God's Word with a marriage. Could God be trying to tell us more than meets the eye of the casual observer in this story? Josh McDowell wrote: "Humankind is not limited in our modes of expression; there is no reason to suppose that God is limited to one style or literary genre in his communication to man."[2] There are times that historical realities presented in God's Word are also metaphorical in meaning, and we commonly refer to these as types, and we even categorize the study of these occurrences as typology. We may see a good example of this in the stories of Joseph or Solomon.

Joseph was rejected by his brothers, but God had chosen him to rule over and deliver his brothers. They never thought that they would ever bow before him, but they did. Israel and the world do not think that they will ever bow before the Lord Jesus Christ, but they will. The Apostle Paul wrote:

> Wherefore God also hath highly exalted him, and given him a name which is above every name: That at the name of Jesus every knee should bow, of things in heaven, and things in earth, and things under the earth; and that every tongue should confess that Jesus Christ is Lord, to the glory of God the Father.
>
> Philippians 2:9–11, KJV

In the first part of his reign, Solomon was a metaphorical picture of the Messiah or a type of the coming Messiah, and in the last part of his reign he was a metaphorical picture of the antichrist or a type of the coming antichrist. A type in this sense is a person or thing in the Old Testament that foreshadows, pictures, or points to something in the New Testament. This being said, and understanding that the Old Testament is pointing to the New, we must ask ourselves: "Is it merely an accident or a coincidence that God's Word begins with marriage and ends with marriage?" Maybe there is more to this.

At that particular time in history, before chapter three of Genesis, God could still say that everything was very good! So, if before the fall God had said that it was very good, what changed? God had not changed! But now Adam and Eve were trying to hide, and when they were confronted by God, they started making excuses, refusing to take responsibility for their own actions. It doesn't seem like much has changed over the years. People still want to blame everyone else for their own mistakes and failures, and the lawyers just love it. In this particular instance, Adam even blamed God! Adam said: "The woman whom thou gavest to be with me, she gave me of the tree, and I did eat" (Genesis 3:12).

Is God trying to reveal something to his people by beginning his Word with a picture of marriage? Alfred Edersheim writes:

> It almost seems as if the relationship of Husband and Bride between Jehovah and his people, so frequently insisted upon, not only in the Bible, but in Rabbinic writings, had always been standing out in the background. Thus the bridal pair on the marriage-day symbolized the union of God with Israel.[3]
>
> Edersheim, 353

Referring later to Adam and Eve's wedding, Edersheim writes: "To use the bold allegory of the times, God himself had spoken the words of blessing over the cup at the union of our first parents, when Michael and Gabriel acted as groomsmen, and the angelic choir sang the wedding hymn." [4] This is not found in the Bible, but it paints a beautiful picture. God was preparing for a covenant relationship with his people that should have been familiar to them from the beginning. God desires to have a life-long and then eternal relationship with all who will come to him of their own free will. God does not do shotgun weddings! He wants to communicate with his people and share their lives, but he never forces himself on anyone. God wants to be with his people when they are facing difficulties and stand beside them to help them through grief and pain, but he also wants to share their joy. Couples who find themselves in a healthy relationship want to spend time together and do things together. They don't spend their time looking for ways to escape one another, and although in human relationships time apart might actually be therapeutic at times, we must remember the promise that Jesus left us: "I am with you alway, even unto the end of the world" (Matthew 28:20).

Here's a lesson that everyone needs to learn about God. He is never surprised. He does not react to our actions and failures. He is proactive! He knows us better than we know ourselves, and he has always had a plan for our redemption. Even before there was any sin, God had a plan for the deliverance of the world from sin. He had this planned from the foundation of the world. The Apostle John wrote:

> The beast that thou sawest was, and is not; and shall ascend out of the bottomless pit, and go into perdition: and they that dwell on the earth shall wonder, whose names are not written in the book of life from the foundation of the world, when they behold the beast that was, and is not, and yet is.
>
> Revelation 17:8

Jesus spoke of a kingdom that was prepared from the foundation of the world as he explained the judgment of the sheep and goats in Matthew 25:34. Revelation 13:8 speaks of "the lamb slain from the foundation of the world." I have to conclude that God has had a plan from before the very beginning, and he has used every means possible to reveal his love, his will, and his plan for humanity's deliverance. He demonstrated his power in delivering Israel from bondage in Egypt, and I believe that this whole historical event was also a picture of something better that was yet to come. For example, God told Moses, "I will raise them up a Prophet from among their brethren, like unto thee, and will put my words in his mouth; and he shall speak unto them all that I shall command him" (Deuteronomy 18:18). Jesus fulfilled this prophecy, but for the most part, Israel did not listen; however, we need to remember that all the early converts to Christianity were Hebrews, and there is an epistle in the New Testament named "Hebrews." The Apostle Paul wrote: "For I am not ashamed of the gospel of Christ: for it is the power of God unto salvation to every one that believeth; to the Jew first, and also to the Greek" (Romans 1:16).

We have to think of God and heaven in human terms, simply because that is the only way that we can understand, because we are human. God knows our plight. So, he explains and reveals himself and his plans through things that are familiar to us. Look at all the parables that Jesus used to illustrate God's will and the kingdom to his followers while at the same time veiling the truth from his enemies. The truth was so veiled in some of these parables that when his disciples were alone with him later, they asked him to explain. God understands our situation so well that he knew the only way he could ever really help us to understand was for him to leave heaven and become one of us.

If, as Dr. John Gray says, men and women need to be aware of their differences in order to properly communicate, then shouldn't humans also remember the differences between themselves and God? If "men are from Mars, and women are from Venus" as far as communication goes, we would do well to remember that God is from heaven, and he exists everywhere. He understands everything and knows everything. Why do we not listen to his advice more intently and heed that advice? Why aren't more people paying attention? Perhaps it is because they want to be in charge of their own lives and be their own god.

Dr. Gray says: "Clearly recognizing and respecting these differences dramatically reduce confusion when dealing with the opposite sex."[5] Dr. Gray speaks of the differences between men and women that we sometimes overlook and thereby create communication blocks that seem insurmountable. He says that when the *Venusians* and the *Martians* first came together that everything was wonderful and beautiful, but one day they were both affected by earth's atmosphere and both groups developed "a peculiar kind of amnesia—*selective amnesia!*"[6] If an imperfect human like Dr. Gray could use the metaphor of Martians and Venusians, it seems quite likely that God could easily use various metaphors to reveal his truth and his plans for us. It seems that at times we all tend to display this type of amnesia, and all too often, it is an amnesia that chooses to forget the Creator. The real reason that we develop this listening disorder and selective memory is that we tend to focus only on what interests us, and the things that interest women do not always interest men, and the things that God considers important do not always seem important to people.

My thought on this problem of differences that cause confusion is that if men and women have difficulty communicating and have an intense need to understand one another, how much more difficult it is for us to understand the differences between us and God? We were totally without hope of understanding anything about him until he became one of us. He has been and still is trying to communicate with us on a level that we can understand. He chose the metaphor of marriage to reveal the type of relationship that he wants to have with us, but this relationship is fraught with perils just like a marriage relationship between a man and a woman.

Lewis Chafer wrote: "In contrast with Israel, who is the unfaithful wife of Jehovah, the church is pictured in the New Testament as the virgin bride awaiting the coming of her Bridegroom (2 Corinthians 11:2)."[7] So, there is a tremendous need for communication and understanding. God understands completely, but we do not. That's our problem. We need to learn his language and listen with our hearts through the power of his Holy Spirit! Paul wrote: "But God hath revealed them unto us by his Spirit: for the Spirit searcheth all things, yea, the deep things of God" (I Corinthians 2:10).

If husbands and wives have difficulty communicating, should we expect communication with God to be easy? We will discuss the real communication gap that exists between us and God in the next chapter. Men and women are different, and they tend to communicate differently. Recognizing and respecting our differences will reduce confusion when dealing with the opposite sex.[8] We should also come to recognize and respect the differences that we have with God and learn to respect and consider those differences in order to better understand his plans and his love for us. God knows everything, and nothing can possibly be concealed from him. We, on the other hand, are very short sighted and limited in our knowledge. God has all power, and we have the illusion of power. God is eternal and can be everywhere at the same instant and is completely limitless, but we are limited to time and space. God knows our thoughts, and sometimes our thoughts are not even clear to us. How much do we need him? We need God more that we need the next breath or the next meal or the next drink of water. The only way that we may have a relationship with him is on his terms.

I have heard people say that there are many paths to God. According to the Bible, there is only one way, and that is through faith in the Lord, Jesus Christ. Those who believe in different paths to God generally embrace some form of salvation by works. The old hymn "Jesus Paid It All" has a very biblical message. We owe everything to him. And our only hope may be summed up in the words from the hymn "Rock of Ages": "Nothing in my hand I bring, simply to thy cross I cling." But we need to move on from the beginning of our relationship with Christ and grow and develop by the power of his Spirit and the application of God's Word in our daily lives. We need to mature in Christ and start producing good fruit.

THE KEYS TO COMMUNICATION

It should be clearly obvious that God is misunderstood more often than not. Even Jesus' closest followers did not seem to understand, as even after the resurrection, they asked him if he would at that time "restore again the kingdom to Israel" in Acts 1:6. There are so many different religions in the world today, and we should be able to perceive that they can't all possibly be correct in their assessment or interpretation of God's will and plan for mankind or in how we may possibly speak to God or receive any communication from him. We will not even attempt to go into the many and varied religions that exist in the world; but instead we will focus on God's message in the Bible and what he is attempting to communicate to us for our benefit, specifically through the metaphorical picture of marriage and divorce as presented in the Holy Bible.

God created this world, and all was originally good and perfect. Man's decision to disobey the Word of God, or *sin*, has devastated that perfect creation, and the effects of sin continue to do harm. Environmentalists continually point to humanity as the source of pollution and destruction of the planet, and I must agree with them to a certain point, but most of them do not understand the true meaning of their own statements, since most of them believe that man simply evolved over millions of years without any divine intervention. Humanity's sin has produced an environmentally devastating moral pollution worse than all the physical pollution in the world ever could. How can anyone ever hope to communicate with God or even understand anything about his creation if they do not believe that he exists? Clearly, this is impossible, unless the Creator steps into his creation and reveals himself. And that is exactly what he has done.

What does God want us to do? Why are we here? These questions have continually perplexed humanity, and the perception of one's particular answer to these questions shapes a person's destiny. I obviously believe that there is a God, and will therefore approach these questions from that perspective. I believe that the Bible teaches categorically that God loves us and desires a very close and intimate relationship with each of us. In order for us to understand the type of relationship that God desires, he uses the picture of marriage to reveal his love and concern for all of us, but divorce also comes into the picture. He wants to be like a loving husband to his people. He wants to protect and provide for us, and he alone has the power to preserve the relationship.

What is required of those whom he calls? Dietrich Bonhoeffer would tell us that God expects us to come and die to ourselves, giving up everything that was before and looking forward to the completely new existence that he provides through our obedience. He writes: "The cross is laid on every Christian. The first Christ-suffering which every man must experience is the call to abandon the attachments to this world."[9] He does say, however: "Obedience to the call of Jesus never lies within our own power."[10] The Apostle Paul said of his own life in Christ: "I am crucified with Christ; nevertheless I live; yet not I, but Christ liveth in me: and the life which I now live in the flesh I live by the faith of the Son of God, who loved me, and gave himself for me" (Galatians 2:20). Remember that there is a need to forsake all others for Christ, and that really means all others, including yourself.

This commitment of one's self completely to God in Christ Jesus is a prerequisite for a person to have any possibility of any effective communication with God. The Apostle Paul wrote: "But the natural man receiveth not the things of the Spirit of God: for they are foolishness unto him: neither can he know them, because they are spiritually discerned" (I Corinthians 2:14). Without a personal relationship with God, it is impossible to completely understand the things that God reveals through his Spirit to those who come to him by faith. This may be the main reason that so many seem to be confused about God's revelation of himself to mankind. If we do not approach the Word through the eyes of faith, it becomes an enigma that we can never truly comprehend, and we must learn to listen intently with the ears of our hearts.

Would or should a person take advice from someone about marriage if the one offering the advice has never been married? Consider the plight of Catholic priests giving marital advice to parishioners when they have never been blessed within a marriage relationship themselves. Sure, they may have spent years studying and reading about marriage and the difficulties that one might encounter, but they have not had to live it. Would you like your next pilot to be a man or woman who has spent years studying how to fly but has never actually been in an airplane? Would or should any parent place much stock in advice from someone who has never been completely committed to a parental position day in and day out and faced with the same challenges and difficulties that they are facing? It was easy for Job's friends to stand outside his personal suffering and offer advice and possible solutions, but they weren't the ones with boils all over their bodies. They had no idea what Job was experiencing or why! What about God? He has definitely experienced the challenges of both marriage and parenthood. He continually tries to direct us as a loving Father, and he relates to Israel and the church through the metaphor of marriage. In Jeremiah 3:13–14, we read: "Turn O backsliding children, saith the Lord: for I am married unto you: and I will take you one of a city, and two of a family, and I will bring you to Zion: and I will give you pastors according to mine heart, which shall feed you with knowledge and understanding." It certainly sounds like God wants us to understand, but we have to listen through the spiritual ears that he has given to us and consider the context in which he speaks. Christl Maier writes:

In the context of ancient Israel and its honor-shame system, the ideal life of a woman would be to grow up as a virgin in her father's house, to be married to a man after puberty and to have a lot of children, especially sons. A woman's sexual relationship to any man who is not her husband would destroy the honor of the whole family and is, therefore, severely dealt with. [11]

Maier, 96

I don't believe that God was particularly happy about this system or the way that women were treated, but it was the custom of ancient Israel, and God used it to illustrate his point. God is going to severely deal with sin. God approaches us where we are and as we are. Jesus treated women with respect. Even the Apostle Paul, who was thoroughly indoctrinated in Judaism and Hebraic tradition, would write: "There is neither Jew nor Greek, there is neither bond nor free, there is neither male nor female: for ye are all one in Christ Jesus" (Galatians 3:28).

Have you ever listened to someone's account of an event in their lives and failed to understand their joviality or concern and then been hit with the words: "I guess you had to be there"? In order to understand the things of God and have an open channel of communication with him, *you have to be there.* Everyone who will know God must take the leap of faith that he is and that Christ is the Lord. Jesus said: "I am the way, the truth, and the life: no man cometh unto the Father, but by me" (John 14:6). Many people want to ask God questions and, in a sense, call him on the carpet over issues that we all face in this world. Now, there is a communication gap! God does not have to answer to us about anything. He is God, and we are not. God is simply waiting for people to humble themselves and come to him for direction and comfort, but many are very angry, and their pride keeps them from the truth.

So, just what are these keys to communication that open the doors to our own understanding? Part of the answer is humility and faith! We may see a terrible picture of what separates too many people from God in C. S. Lewis' *The Great Divorce*. In this book, the ghost of an Episcopal priest who doesn't believe in a literal heaven or hell is heard talking to an almost blindingly white spirit who is trying to convince the priest to follow him to heaven, but his intellect and pride keep him from following.[12] A person does not have to assassinate his or her intellect to come to Christ, but one must humbly submit to the Father's will, and many times the intellect blocks the path to humility. There are many more examples of things that block the path to God in Lewis' story, but the keys to heaven seem to be faith, humility, hope, and a love that is not self-centered or self-serving. It also becomes evident that *The Great Divorce* is about humanity's divorce of God and the truth. Someone once observed that if a person is feeling farther and farther from God, they should ask themselves: "Who moved?" Be assured, it was not God that somehow drifted away from us. In the conclusion to this story, the priest's ghost says: "… I should want a guarantee that you are taking me to a place where I shall find a wider sphere of usefulness—and scope for talents that God has given me—and an atmosphere of

free inquiry—in short, all that one means by civiliza-
tion and–er–the spiritual life."[13] To which the White
Spirit replies:

> "No," said the other, "I can promise you none of
> those things. No sphere of usefulness: you are not
> needed there at all. No scope for your talents:
> only forgiveness for having perverted them. No
> atmosphere of inquiry, for I will bring you to the
> land not of questions but of answers, and you shall
> see the face of God." The priest answers: "For me
> there is no such thing as a final answer."[14]

Lewis, 36

The Bible teaches that there is a final answer, and
it may be found in the shed blood of Jesus Christ and
the power of his resurrection. But as Ripley has said so
many times: "Believe it or not." God has promised to
never leave us nor forsake us, but here we see a picture
of continual enticement to salvation that is refused. *The
Great Divorce* is a case of man divorcing God, not the
other way around. God is definitely the guiltless party.

Humanity is still trying to distance itself from God
and declare him irrelevant. We hear the mantra being
proclaimed around every corner in America today:
"Separation of Church and State." These are words
that are repeated with great authority, and if you think
about it, a godless state seems to be the ideal for many
people. These words are not, however, to be found in
the Constitution, The Bill of Rights, or the Declaration
of Independence; however, I actually agree with the
idea of separation, though these words are not used of

church and state as described in the first amendment to the *United States Constitution.* The first amendment says:

> Congress shall make no law respecting an estab-
> lishment of religion, or prohibiting the free exer-
> cise thereof; or abridging the freedom of speech,
> or of the press; or the right of the people peace-
> ably to assemble, and to petition the Government
> for a redress of grievances.[15]

> U. S. Constitution, Amendment 1

The founding fathers clearly did not want the state to establish a national religion, but they clearly desired freedom of religion, which would be different from their current and previous experiences. They had expe-rienced religious tolerance and discovered that it wasn't very tolerant, and what they truly desired was religious freedom. In his famous letter to the Danbury Baptist Association, President Thomas Jefferson used the metaphor of "a wall of separation between church and state."[16] The people did not desire freedom from reli-gion but freedom to worship or not to worship accord-ing to an individual's conscience and convictions. This is also in line with God's will for the world. Remember, God does not force himself on anyone but offers free-dom for individual choice, and neither should earthly governments force anyone to a particular religion.

Here is another part of the key. We must receive Christ of our own free will. No other person, orga-nization, church, religion or religious leader, or even government can make this decision for us. The Bible tells us that Jesus came unto his own people. His message was directed toward Israel, but the apostle John writes:

> He came unto his own, and his own received him not. But as many as received him, to them gave he the power to become the sons of God, even to them that believe on his name: Which were born, not of blood, nor of the will of the flesh, nor of the will of man, but of God.
>
> John 1:11–13

You may wonder how it is possible to receive Christ, and the answer is fairly simple. The Apostle Paul wrote in Romans 10:9: "That if thou shalt confess with your mouth the Lord Jesus, and believe in thine heart that God hath raised him from the dead, thou shalt be saved." A few verses later, in Romans 10:13, Paul says: "For whosoever shall call upon the name of the Lord shall be saved." People's lack of humility and lack of faith cause them to seek to do something to assist the Lord in their deliverance, but Christ has already done it all. The debt is paid in full, and to insist that Christ's death and resurrection are not enough is to insult and to declare as insufficient the sacrifice of God's only begotten Son. Everyone must approach God on God's terms, without insisting upon adding anything or subtracting anything. This requires a spirit of humility and admitting one's own inadequacy. According to Dr. Gray, human nature might make this very difficult. Speaking of men in relationships, he says: "A man's deepest fear is that he is not good enough or that he is incompetent."[17] Jesus said: "Verily I say unto you, whosoever will not receive the kingdom as a little child, he shall not enter therein" (Mark 10:15). *As a little child*—this is a simile that refers to humility and childlike trust. Jesus was not saying that only children could enter the kingdom, but he was telling us to humbly trust and believe. Scripture clearly teaches that the only way a human can understand the things of the Spirit is by first being born of the spirit. How can anyone hope to understand the infinite glory of God apart from God's own indwelling presence to guide and reveal truth? It can't be done!

The key to experiencing the opportunity of communication with God then comes through commitment of one's self to God by faith in the atoning work of the Lord, Jesus Christ, in all humility, understanding that Christ has paid the total price of your redemption from sin and death, and Christ, through the sending of the Holy Spirit, has provided the means by which one may now communicate with God on a personal level. If, however, you feel the line of communication is broken, God is not the problem. A person must remain true to God as a bride should be true to her husband. A new believer needs to strive to retain a humble spirit and obey God's will in every aspect of his or her life. We have been purchased with the blood of Christ, and we cannot compartmentalize our lives, allotting a little time for God and the rest for ourselves while expecting him to bless us in all things. Proverbs 3:5–6 says: "Trust in the Lord with all thine heart; and lean not unto thine own understanding. In all thy ways acknowledge him, and he shall direct thy paths."

Another of the keys to communication with God involves our own availability. If a couple gets married and then they go their own ways for weeks, months, or years on end, what kind of relationship will they have? Many marriages fail simply because husbands and wives seem to grow apart. They don't have time for one another because of work, children, or even church, and they develop totally different interests as they spend more and more time apart. Someone once said that absence makes the heart grow fonder, but if a spouse is absent long enough, my experience says that absence will sometimes make the heart grow fonder for someone else who is paying attention. Here is a picture of what God has continually had to deal with since the beginning of time. People simply get interested in other things and become so busy that they do not have time for God. Why then, did God choose to demonstrate his relationship with Israel and the church through the metaphor of marriage? It seems fairly obvious to me. We may observe the joy in a committed marriage relationship and the sorrow and pain produced by a failing marriage. Sadly, it seems there are more failing marriages than there are good ones.

God wants to communicate to us as clearly as possible, and he desires a covenant relationship that involves commitment, caring, and continuing love and communion. He wants to speak to our hearts on a daily basis, and he desires an ongoing dialog that will work for our benefit both now and throughout all eternity. He wants a relationship that resembles a truly happy and healthy marriage. He desires a big family that is brought together through selfless love and increased in size through adoption of sons and daughters. No one is physically born into God's family, but they are "born again" spiritually and adopted by the Father. Jesus told Nicodemus: "Marvel not that I said unto thee, Ye must be born again. The wind bloweth where it listeth, and thou hearest the sound thereof, but canst not tell whence it cometh, and whither it goeth: so is everyone that is born of the Spirit" (John 3:7–8). And Paul wrote to the church at Rome: "For as many as are led by the Spirit of God, they are the sons of God. For ye have not received the spirit of bondage again to fear; but ye have received the Spirit of adoption, whereby we cry, Abba, Father" (Romans 8:14–15). In a recent article in *Southwestern News,* Thomas White says: "Unfortunately, many understand the theological concept of adoption less than they understand the cultural concept."[18] A few lines later he writes: "Each believer in Christ has been adopted by God, and to understand the gospel completely, you must comprehend the theology of adoption."[19] We might also add that it is unfortunate that too many do not understand the cultural concept of marriage any more than they understand the relationship that God desires to have with his called out people, even though he has repeatedly used the metaphor of marriage to describe and reveal it. Since we are considering God's use of metaphor, let's create one of our own.

God is, in a sense, trying to build a work of priceless art, but he is dealing with an unwilling canvas and rebellious stone. Consider Leonardo da Vinci's world famous "Mona Lisa," or *La Giaconda,* that is displayed in the Louvre in Paris, France. What if every time

Leonardo da Vinci tried to apply the brush to the poplar panel he chose to use for this painting, it moved away from him? How could he have ever completed this wonderful masterpiece? When my family and I toured the Louvre in December of 2003, we saw hundreds of beautiful works of art, but when we arrived before this painting, although in comparison to the many other paintings it was relatively small, it suddenly became the biggest thing in the entire gallery.

What if every time Michelangelo had reached out to remove a piece of marble that was concealing the statue of "David," the stone drew back in fear of the sculptor? When we stood before this beautiful piece of art in Florence, Italy, it was simply amazing. You could see the veins in the hands with every attention to detail, except, of course, that it was not anatomically correct. With all the attention to detail on this sculpture, including the sling draped over his left shoulder, it is not clear exactly why Michelangelo produced a statue representing the young Jewish king in the nude as a male subject that had not been circumcised.

When we visited Rome, we took a tour of the Vatican and had the opportunity to stand in the Sistine Chapel and be totally overwhelmed by the beauty of our surroundings. Looking up to see the famous fresco of God reaching out to Adam was awesome, and I remember saying to my wife: "I thought that it would have been bigger." It was just one of many panels with biblical illustrations that pictured the history of God's dealings with his people. But what if every time Michelangelo started to work on the frescos on the ceiling of the Sistine Chapel, the ceiling moved away from him? He was already resentful about having to produce these works of art for the Pope. How long would he have persisted? This is a picture of what God faces every time he reaches out to touch someone's life but without the resentment. He wants to create something wonderful and new, but his canvas, his poplar panel, or his marble blocks are pulling away from him, but God waits patiently for them to come back to him.

If you think these art metaphors are far-fetched, consider the following. Paul says that we are God's farm and God's house. These are all metaphors to help us understand that we should allow God to work in our lives and place us or plant us as he sees fit. "For we are labourers together with God: ye are God's husbandry, ye are God's building" (I Corinthians 3:9). Peter says that we are stones used by God to build a spiritual house. I wonder where he got an idea like that! Do you suppose he was referring to something that Jesus said to him? "Ye also, as lively stones, are built up a spiritual house, a holy priesthood, to offer up spiritual sacrifices, acceptable to God by Jesus Christ" (I Peter 2:5). "Therefore if any man be in Christ, he is a new creature: old things are passed away; behold, all things are become new" (I Corinthians 5:17). If God is creating a building and we are the stones, why do we resist his attempts to place us where we will best fit in to create a masterpiece for all eternity? If we are supposed to be new creatures or new creations, what is hindering the progress? God is not the problem. He is patient, considerate, and kind. We are the clay, and he is the potter, and just as Jeremiah observed, he can make us as it seems "good" to him. (Jeremiah 18:4). We don't turn the potter's wheel as he molds us for his use. He does it all. We simply need to allow him to shape us according to his desires for whatever purpose he desires.

The "Mona Lisa" did not paint herself. The statue of "David" did not carve itself. The ceiling of the Sistine Chapel did not paint itself. The church needs to learn to "be still" like these inanimate objects and submit to the hand of the Master. "Be still, and know that I am God: I will be exalted among the heathen, I will be exalted in the earth" (Psalm 46:10). In an extremely mobile age, being still is sometimes very difficult, and when we are still, we are watching sports, television shows, or movies. When will we learn to actually set aside time just for God and listen to what he has to say?

Trying to teach sixth grade boys has taught me a lot about the frustration that God must feel with people. These boys are at the half-way point in their public school education, and they are beginning to think that they really know what it's all about. Never mind that they don't even know what "it" is, but they think they know more or just as much as most adults. Bear in mind that I am talking about a specific group of sixth grade boys and not all of them, but I see a picture of rebellion and disobedience from a group of boys who don't know much about life, God, or anything for that matter, and they will not take the time to listen to someone who does. This is the exact situation that God faces every moment with his rebellious creation. This book deals with word pictures that God has taken great care in putting together for our benefit, and spiritual education. Very few have even pointed it out except for the mention of a thread or a theme in Scripture. The biggest problem that I face with sixth grade boys is getting them to be still and listen, and God has the same problem with people. God holds the secrets to the universe that he created. Why won't we just take time to listen to what he wants us to know?

ORIGIN OF DIVORCE AND THE ONGOING PROBLEM

Addressing the Pharisees concerning a tricky question about the grounds for divorce and referring to Moses, Jesus said: "For the hardness of your hearts he gave you this precept. But from the beginning of the creation God made them male and female" (Mark 10:5b-6). Jesus then quotes Adam's statement or prophecy about leaving father and mother and cleaving to one's wife, becoming one flesh. Jesus had more to say about this in Matthew 19:8–12. Because of the two schools of thought about grounds for divorce, it didn't matter what Jesus might have claimed as grounds for divorce; they would have found fault with his answer. Jesus basically told them that they were the problem. This was not the answer they wanted, and it certainly was not the answer they expected. This is a perfect example of why it is not a good idea to try to live your life guessing or imagining what Jesus would do in various situations.

It is best to simply apply his Word and let his Spirit lead.

The first time we see the mention of "putting away" is in a commandment to the priests not to take a wife who has been put away by another man in Leviticus 21:7. In this same verse, the priests are also told not to take a wife that is profane or a whore. Divorce is first mentioned in Deuteronomy 24:1–4, and it is clearly stated that a man may not take his former wife back if she becomes the wife of another, even if the second husband dies, and the law says that it would be "abomination before the Lord" if that were to happen, and it would "cause the land to sin" because she is defiled. How does this verse apply when we consider God's choice to divorce Israel?

If a man cannot take back his former wife without defiling the land and becoming an abomination, how can God ever take back Israel, since he divorced her, according to Isaiah 50:1 and Jeremiah 3:8? First, we must always remember that God is not a man, even though in Christ, he became a man. God's plan involves the making of a totally new creation in Christ Jesus. God will not take back an idolatrous, unregenerate Israel, but he will take a new bride that is made absolutely glorious and pure through the applied blood of the Lamb. This new bride will include people of the kingdoms of Israel and Judah along with all the other people in the world who will accept the sacrifice of the Savior as atonement or complete payment and covering for their sins. In discussing Ephesians 5:25–33, Lewis Sperry Chafer writes:

> Here the threefold work of Christ is revealed: (a) in his death, "Christ also loved the church and gave himself for it" (Vs. 25); (b) Christ is engaged in the present work, "that he might sanctify and cleanse it with the washing of water by the word" (vs. 26); (c) "that he might present it to himself a glorious church, not having spot, or wrinkle, or any such thing; but that it should be holy and without blemish."[20]

> Chafer, 278

The church is the bride of Christ, and this passage of Scripture begins with, "Husbands, love your wives, even as Christ also loved the church, and gave himself for it" (Ephesians 5:25). Was Ephesians chapter five written simply to try to force modern marriages to fit a first century understanding of the marriage relationship, or was there something more being taught? Pray and then read it again, and decide for yourself. Then pray some more. So, this new bride will be cleansed, glorious, without spot or wrinkle, holy, and without blemish. This would be impossible for a human in dealing with a former wife, but with God, nothing is impossible.

Considering the origin of divorce, we could say that, in a sense, Adam and Eve divorced or "put away" God by refusing to believe and obey his warning concerning the forbidden fruit. They lost their special relationship and ability to serve him by believing the serpent rather than believing God. Divorce, then, actually originated as the result of sin. Marriage is a covenant relationship, and God always deals with his people through a covenant relationship. Going after false gods or tinkering about with the occult, or simply trying to make it on our own, is like the sin of adultery or whoredom. God had entered a covenant relationship with Adam and Eve, and it only had one rule with a clearly stated consequence: Don't eat of the tree of the knowledge of good and evil, or you will die. Soren Kierkegaard wrote:

> The one who truly loves never falls away from love. Yet, is it always possible to prevent a break in a relationship between two persons, especially when the other has given up? One would certainly not think so. Is not one of the two enough to break the relationship? In a certain sense it is so. But if the lover is determined not to fall away from love, he can prevent the break, he can perform this miracle; for if he perseveres, a total break can never really come to be.[21]

> Kierkegaard, 119

It is difficult at times to know whether Kierkegaard is speaking of God or man. Man does not have the capacity or the ability to love like God loves, unless of course, God loves through him. Did Adam and Eve truly understand the concept of love? Do we? It may be argued that even though Jesus said that Moses gave you the precept of divorce, in a sense, it already existed before Moses when Adam and Eve put away their relationship with God by breaking the covenant. Jesus understood the whole concept of divorce completely, but in dealing with the Pharisees, it was best to point to Moses as an example. If you study the passage of Scripture in Mark 10:2–8, you will notice that Christ did point to the beginning when God made them male and female, but he went no further. He had proved his point, and he, the incarnation of love, was standing in their presence while they searched for ways to trap and kill him.

Did Adam and Eve comprehend the meaning of death in a world that had never experienced death? I don't think they had a clue about how extensive the consequences would be or how many would be affected. At this point in time, it really doesn't matter what they understood. They chose to disobey God's only rule that was given for their benefit, and they suffered the consequences. We are still suffering the consequences, but God has provided a way of escape. God has a plan for a holy and completely perfect marriage.

Many see divorce as a way of escape from unhappiness, and they expect to find true happiness, security, and peace of mind in another relationship with something or someone else. Israel had done this in chasing after false gods, worshiping idols, mixing heathen religious practices with their worship of Yahweh, and making alliances with heathen governments, seeking a lasting national security. Rather than trusting in God and giving him the glory, they sought to work things out in their own way. This is how Christian marriages fail today when we forget that we are not alone, but we choose to go it alone. David Gushee writes: "Covenant promises are binding; they restrict our future freedom of action on the basis of our present decision." He then says: "We need symbols and rituals to remind us of all this. We need the structure of covenants, so it is covenants we are given."[22] Like the late W. C. Fields, too many people are looking for loopholes. By the way, Fields didn't find any loopholes in the Bible, because there are none. People seem to always resist what is good for them. But who decides what is good for us? If the God who created us thinks we need covenants, you can bet that we need covenants. But that doesn't keep us from looking for a way out because everything does not always go to suit us. People are influenced greatly by temporary circumstances, and they have a tendency to drift with the fashions and fads of the day. We are confused many times, and we have a tendency to judge everything based on current knowledge with its partial evidence and contemporary thought.

We are becoming a hardened society. Divorce used to carry a stigma in America, but when everyone is doing it, it becomes an accepted practice. There is obviously still a stigma in the church. Many seem to consider the subject taboo. It is interesting that though the metaphor of marriage is discussed at length in the *Dictionary of Biblical Imagery*, that divorce and "putting away" are not discussed at all. Where the word "divorce" or "divorcement" should have been, it skipped from "divine warrior" to "dogs."[23] Perhaps the author of the dictionary did not think there was any imagery involved. This absence of divorce in the dictionary is especially interesting if we consider what Jay Adams says: "In biblical times, how did divorce take place? Interestingly, the scriptures provide more detail about the process of divorce than they do about engagements or wedding ceremonies."[24] The only preaching that many have heard about divorce was very condemning and has offered little comfort to those who have already been divorced. Some even think that divorce will send them to hell. Thank God for grace! Divorce and the way divorced people are treated is a problem, and until we face a problem, we can never deal with it.

For the most part, many churches do not minister to the families that are touched by divorce. Instead, they are suspicious and tend to keep them at arm's length instead of giving them the love and understanding that they need so much. They tend to comfort widows, widowers, and orphans without taking into account the grief experienced by anyone who goes through a divorce. This is a very prevalent problem that can't just be swept under the rug. Ignoring it won't make it go away.

The religion of the Pharisees is sadly still alive and well in the modern Christian church. God is loving and forgiving. He is the God of second chances, but the people who claim to know him and supposedly try to be like him are nothing like the Father, but they could be through his Holy Spirit. Too many are so concerned about being theologically correct that they fail to see God's mission for their lives. They forget the *new commandment* while clinging to the old ones. Jesus said: "A new commandment I give unto you, that ye love one another; as I have loved you, that ye love one another" (John 13:34)

God uses the metaphor of marriage and says: "Love one another." Isn't this clear? Apparently, it isn't. The Apostle Paul told husbands in his Epistle to the Ephesians to love their wives even as Christ loved the church and gave himself for it. Just as husbands are supposed to love their wives, God loves us and has made the ultimate sacrifice for us. We should love God in the same way. But since God is invisible, we might apply the old saying: "Out of sight, out of mind." Is God really out of sight, or are our eyes simply closed? Jesus would say "consider the lilies" or "consider the sparrows." The creation screams with evidence for God, and in a sense, the rocks really do cry out, but very few seem to be listening. If divorce is your goal, just stop listening. It will happen. This is how people divorce God. They just stop listening and ignore all the signs while busying themselves with everyday matters.

What about love? How would God tell us to demonstrate our love for him? Many think that this involves regular church attendance, salvation and baptism, partaking of the Lord's Supper, tithing, praying regularly, reading their Bibles, Bible study, and keeping one's self unspotted by the world. These are all important, but they fall short of God's requirements. A person can do all the above mentioned things and still not be what God wants them to be. Paul wrote to the people of Corinth: "Charity [love] never faileth: but whether there be prophecies, they shall fail; whether there be tongues, they shall cease; whether there be knowledge, it shall vanish away" (I Corinthians 13:8). Of course he closes this chapter with: "the greatest of these is charity [love]" (I Corinthians 13:13b). It is interesting that the King James Version of the Bible repeatedly translates the Greek word *agape* as charity. This is the word that describes the self-sacrificing love that seeks nothing in return, which God has for us. Jesus makes it very clear what he desires from his children that will demonstrate their love for him. He says: "Inasmuch as ye have done it unto the least of these my brethren, ye have done it unto me" (Matthew 25:40). And the other side of the story is: "Inasmuch as ye did it not to one of the least of these, ye did it not to me" (Matthew 25:45). Jesus was talking about feeding the hungry, giving drink to the thirsty, taking in or sheltering strangers, clothing the naked, visiting the sick, and visiting those in prison. He was saying that we should minister to people and thereby demonstrate our love for him. How practical is our Christianity? Are we doing these things, or are we too busy being religious? Religious ritual and ceremony do not impress God.

Bill McCartney, who started Promise Keepers while coaching at the University of Colorado, is a devout Christian, but he was so busy that he was neglecting his marriage. When faced with the pain that he was causing his wife, he agreed to see a Christian counselor. Meeting with this Christian counselor for the first time, Bill said: "He knew who I was. He knew all about Promise Keepers, that was expanding across the nation, going full throttle. He wasn't impressed."[25] God is not at all impressed with how busy we are or even how religious we are. He wants us to love him by loving others. He wants us to take time to communicate with him. Bill has left coaching, and in September 2008, he accepted the positions of CEO and chairman of the board of Promise Keepers.

I heard Charles Stanley say in one of his messages that, at times, the most godly thing that we can do is to take some time and rest, and I agree completely.

God wants us to set things aside so he can get us alone and minister to us, but after we are refreshed, he expects us to minister to others. God especially wants us to give quality time to our spouse, our children, and our church family, but he also wants us to go beyond those boundaries to "the least of these." Many people shunned Charles Stanley when he got divorced a few years ago, and our local Christian radio station refused to carry any of his messages. They have since recanted and are again airing his programs. He's still preaching and teaching, and I praise God for helping him through his times of difficulty and grief. If your wife or husband decides to leave you, that doesn't mean that God will leave you, and it does not mean that God is through with you.

Divorce originated in sin and the hardness of people's hearts. Sin cannot be overcome with more sin. The only way to deal with those who have been divorced is with love, understanding, and grace. If someone is facing the possibility of a failed marriage, they need to seek godly counsel immediately, before it is too late. Divorce continues to demonstrate the weakness of the flesh. Sadly, those who claim to know Christ are affected by divorce as much as or more than those who do not know him. What would you be willing to do to maintain your marriage to the glory of God?

CELIBACY:
OTHER THAN SEX,
WHAT IS MISSING?

The idea that celibacy enhances a person's ability to serve God as a Christian committed to serving God began long after the resurrection of the Lord Jesus Christ and the birth of the church. J. N. D. Kelley writes:

> The monastic ideal, with its summons to throw off the entanglements of ordinary life, not least the attractions of sex, had been sweeping through the Christian east since the beginning of the fourth century; nowhere had it caught on more effectively than in Syria, and nowhere did it assume more bizarre forms.[26]

Kelly, 3

John Chrysostom was born in Antioch, Syria, and he was indoctrinated with these ideas of celibacy and total self-denial throughout his early years. He would later be canonized as a saint in the Roman Catholic Church and was well known for his brilliant oratory skills. As we will see later, he had definite beliefs about the practice of celibacy and separating one's self for ministry.

John Calvin and Martin Luther did not agree often, but when it came to the question of celibacy, they were united.

> Calvin had two reasons in joining with Luther in protesting against the vow of celibacy; the conviction that marriage was a holy institution ordained of God and therefore permitted to all, and the equally strong conviction that marriage was a very necessary human institution if unchastity was to be avoided.[27]
>
> Harkness, 133

If God is, and I believe that he is, trying to teach the church something through the relationship of marriage, wouldn't it make sense that the devil would do everything in his power to pervert and even forbid marriage? The Apostle Paul warned Timothy:

> Now the Spirit speaketh expressly, that in the latter times some will depart from the faith, giving heed to seducing spirits, and doctrines of devils; Speaking lies in hypocrisy; having their conscience seared with a hot iron; forbidding to marry, and commanding to abstain from meats, which God hath created to be received with thanksgiving of them which believe and know the truth.
>
> I Timothy 4:1–3

If Paul was describing false teachers in the *latter times,* as he says, and he included *forbidding to marry* as a sign of these false teachers, why do some Christian leaders still forbid marriage and use Paul's letter to Corinth as a proof text?

Writing to a friend concerning his choice to leave the monastery and possibly even get married, John Chrysostom is reported to have responded with the following:

> John upbraids his young friend with "erasing his name from the list of brothers" and "trampling on the contract he had entered into with Christ." Marriage, he concedes, may in general be honourable, but for Theodore it would amount to adultery since he has "joined himself to the heavenly bridegroom."[28]
>
> Kelly, 23

Theodore repented and returned to the monastery after thinking about what John had written to him, and this letter became famous. Kelly says: "Serious Christians a couple of generations later were filled with admiration for his letter, the pious Sozomen exclaiming that in both diction and sentiments it was more divine than the mind of man could conceive."[29] Sozomen should have been more careful with his praise of Chrysostom's letter and his claim of divine inspiration. Chrysostom, because of his own monastic lifestyle, was very biased on this subject. He praised the choice of celibacy and Kelly says: "By contrast, the best he can say of marriage is that it is, 'for those who choose to use it rightly, a haven of chastity, preventing human nature from relapsing into bestiality.'" [30] How would you like to have this guy for a marriage counselor? As to whether or not one should place a great deal of faith in Chrysostom, we might want to consider another of his quotes. He said:

> The Jews souls have become the dwelling-places of demons: not surprisingly, since they are "Christ-killers" (*Christoktonoi*) who did not shrink from slaying the Lord. God himself speaking through the prophets has branded their worship as abominable; they themselves should be shunned as a filthy plague threatening the entire world. [31]
>
> Kelly, 64

This does not sound like it came from a "golden mouth" to me but from a potty mouthed anti-Semite of the first order. And it should be made perfectly clear that the Jews were not responsible for the death of Christ. It was sin, yours and mine, that cried out for his death on the cross. Our sin nailed him there, and had he not died, we would still be in our sin, and this world would be a completely different place. Had he not offered himself, this world might not even exist at this point.

It seems strange to me that the monastic lifestyle is rationalized through the writings of Paul, but they only seem to rely on I Corinthians chapter 7, and they seem to overlook or simply ignore Paul's statements concerning the qualifications of bishops in I Timothy 3:2 and elders in Titus 1:6. In both I Timothy and

Titus, Paul says that bishops and elders should be the husband of one wife. Again, we must ask ourselves: "Why?" Why would anyone want to pervert the Word of God and establish a ritual lifestyle that forbids marriage? This was not something new. The Essenes had lived a monastic lifestyle in the Qumran community, but there were also others of this cult that were married. If one were to live in Qumran, he would have to live a monastic life, but if he chose to live outside the Qumran community, he could marry. The choice belonged to the individual. Based upon the information in the Dead Sea Scrolls, the Essenes had two sets of community rules for this very purpose. Perhaps the devil wants us to miss the marvelous message that God is trying to deliver to his people through the marriage relationship.

What is missing from a life of celibacy besides sex? Gary Thomas says: "Not only can being married remind us of God's nature and character, but it also reminds us of his moral claims on our lives."[32] In a monastic lifestyle, one misses the opportunity to grow in many ways. They miss the opportunity to share their lives and ministry with another person that God has prepared for that very purpose. They miss the joy of raising their own children and training them in the Lord's will. They miss the opportunity to mirror the relationship that God desires to have with his people. They miss the joy of oneness that pictures our oneness with God. But Gary Thomas warns the married couple: "There are no lessons to be learned when a man dominates his wife. There are no inspiring examples to emulate when a woman manipulates her husband."[33]

The monastics overlook the power of the Lord's statement as it applies to married couples: "That if two of you shall agree on earth as touching anything that they shall ask, it shall be done for them of my Father which is in heaven" (Matthew 18:19). However, Peter warns about hindering one's prayers if a man does not dwell with his wife "according to knowledge" in I Peter 3:7, and he should know, because he was married. The man that the Catholic Church claims was the first Pope was married. Imagine that! Matthew 8:14, Mark 1:30, and Luke 4:38 all record the healing of Peter's wife's mother by the Lord Jesus Christ.

But is there something more to be learned in I Peter 3:7? If marriage is a metaphor designed to help us understand the relationship that God desires to have with us both individually and corporately, what might hinder our prayer life and what would be the significance of that hindered prayer life? If we can do nothing apart from Jesus Christ and the power of the Holy Spirit, how important is an unhindered prayer life? Without prayer, we are totally without power or hope, and we are unable to fulfill any of God's plans for us, because everything depends on what he does in and through us, and nothing that we do in our flesh is pleasing to him. The marriage relationship, as we have already seen, is a picture of the intimacy that God desires to have with his people, but if there is no intimacy and prayer lives are hindered within a marriage, how much more is this amplified within the church body as people bicker and gossip and generally do not even seem to enjoy one another's company?

God has called us to be a family, but the broken

families that fill the pews teach us nothing of the relationship that God desires to have with all of us. Since judgment must begin in the house of the Lord, it's time we considered our own sin rather than pointing out the sin of the world. Since the church is referred to as the bride of Christ and we are supposed to all be one in Christ Jesus, should we not make a habit of working on our relationships with one another? Husbands and wives are supposed to be one flesh, and the church is supposed to be the body of Christ, and he only has one body. Prayers may be hindered because of problems within a marriage but also because of strained relationships within the church.

In Matthew 5:23, Jesus said: "Therefore if thou bring thy gift to the altar, and there rememberest that thy brother hath ought against thee, Leave there thy gift before the altar, and go thy way; first be reconciled to thy brother, and then come and offer thy gift." If Peter is telling us that we need to improve our marriages in order to improve our prayer lives, wouldn't it follow that if we want to improve our prayer lives we need to start by improving our relationships within the body of Christ as well? This appears to be obvious.

Later in his book, Thomas refers to Matthew 5:23, but he says something that I'm not sure I completely understand. He writes: "I'm not obligated to be in a relationship with everybody, so there's nothing inherently wrong with simply 'sidestepping' people who really raise your blood pressure."[34] Please don't get the wrong idea. I highly recommend Gary Thomas's book, *Sacred Marriage*. But if these people are a part of the body of Christ, wouldn't it be more sensible to simply learn to agreeably disagree while continuing to love them? After all, Christ said that we are even supposed to love our enemies. If, as he says, marriage forces us into the intense act of reconciliation, shouldn't being a part of God's family do the same? If we need to do the necessary relational work in order to proceed to unity within a marriage, what excuses us from not doing the same within the body of Christ? However, there are a few that attend church that refuse to accept reconciliation, but we should still love them and pray for them. Perhaps this is the type of person that Gary Thomas is referring to, but don't take this as a blanket excuse for avoiding anyone you don't particularly like. Again, maybe God is trying to teach us something more. If, as Thomas says, "The institution of marriage is designed to force us to become reconcilers,"[35] shouldn't we carry this ministry of reconciliation beyond our own families to the church and to the world? However, in Romans 16:17, Paul clearly warns about those who cause divisions and offences contrary to the gospel and tells us to avoid them. If these are the types of people that Thomas suggests we avoid, he is scripturally correct, but people that are just hard to love or difficult to approach are not included in this scriptural mandate.

Concerning the choice of a celibate lifestyle, Gary Thomas wrote: "Although Christianity was born out of Judaism, a religion in which marriage was considered a religious duty (one Rabbi suggested that a man who does not marry is not fully a man.) ..."[36] A forced celibacy on all who would dedicate themselves to the service of Christ is unscriptural and unnatural as well. It is the fulfillment of the prophecy concerning false teachers that will come in the latter days. It comes out of a belief in salvation by works and is supposed to require the celibate to remain pure in deed and in thought. It is totally unrealistic and has created as many problems as it has avoided. Consider the constant rumors and realities of abuse of children and sexual sin. It prevents the priest from understanding the joys and difficulties of marriage, but it does not prevent sexual misconduct. Celibacy by choice is a different matter, and the Scriptures recognize this ability as a gift from God. In Matthew 19:10–11, Jesus discusses this with his disciples: "His disciples say unto him, If the case of the man be so with his wife, it is not good to marry. But he said unto them, All men cannot receive this saying, save they to whom it is given."

What may we learn from marriage? We learn to share everything, just as we are to share everything with God. We learn to make sacrifices just as God sacrificed his Son for us. We learn to become "one" with another very special human being just as Christ desires us to be one with him. We learn to be considerate just as Christ was considerate of us and all those he ministered to in his earthly life. If God is trying to teach us about a relationship that he desires to have with us through the metaphor of marriage, how may we fully grasp these insights apart from the personal commitment and the personal experience of marriage? There is no doubt that it may be accomplished, but only from the outside looking in at someone else's marriage. Remember the old saying: I guess you just had to be there. How important are the examples set by Christians in marriage?

If you consider that your relationship with your

husband or wife is supposed to be a representation of the relationship of Christ with the church, how much attention should you give to that relationship? How important is it? I believe that nothing but your own personal relationship with God in Christ Jesus is more important! If we can't love the body of Christ, our wives, or our husbands, how can we claim to love God? The Apostle John wrote: "If a man say, I love God, and hateth his brother, he is a liar; for he that loveth not his brother whom he hath seen, how can he love God whom he hath not seen?" (I John 4:20). Remember about serving *the least of these, my brethren.* When you do good to anyone in the name of Christ, you are blessed by providing a blessing, and according to Matthew 10:42 or Mark 9:41, you will not lose your reward. But as Randy Philips wrote: "There's no commitment to change when men have a comfortable Christianity that makes no demands on their lives."[37] He could have said the same about commitment to change within a marriage. It is easy to become comfortable and do nothing, and many preachers and teachers today are proclaiming the need for the church members to get out of their comfort zone and start truly serving God. Within the church, just as in a marriage, just because you may feel that everything is going fine and there is very little that needs to be done does not mean that your feelings are correct, and these feelings of security will ultimately cause you grief. We shouldn't just trust our feelings. We should trust and obey God's Word. If we choose to simply follow our feelings or follow the doctrines of men, we will miss the joy, the experiences, and the power with which God desires to bless us. Too many people have adopted the attitude that something can't be wrong if it feels right. That is one of the dumbest things I have ever heard! It might feel right to commit adultery, but it is not ever right. It might feel right at the time to commit premeditated murder, but no matter how one rationalizes his position, it is sin. It might even feel right at a particular time to steal, but God's Word says that it is wrong. How in the world did Robin Hood ever become a hero? Perhaps it was because people thought that stealing felt right at the time and that there was no other way to handle the situation, but they were wrong. We wonder why our young people are confused, but when you consider their heroes and what they are exposed to on a daily basis, it begins to make sense.

DESIRED RELATIONSHIP

God desires a relationship with his church that is like a perfect marriage! The church is supposed to be the bride of Christ. *The Dictionary of Biblical Imagery* says: "Throughout the Bible, God's relationship to his people is pictured as a marriage. In this metaphor, God is the husband and his people are the wife."[38] To help us understand the imagery, the dictionary also says: "In Israelite society the man was head of the household, so within the marriage metaphor, it is understandable that God is cast in the role of the husband."[39] God wants a relationship in which he is the head and we are in submission to his perfect will. The picture, then, of a Christian wife being in submission to her husband would have the effect of demonstrating and revealing the type of relationship that God desires to have with us; however, it must be remembered that there are no earthly husbands with God's insights, understanding, or compassion. God presents a perfect picture of a perfect relationship between himself and all believers. Trying to apply this in an earthly marriage has serious limitations due again to the fallen state of humanity and the weakness of the flesh. Both man and wife are imperfect, and we must also note that God is revealing truth to a fallen world within the limited understanding of a relationship between a husband and wife as it was understood in Hebrew history.

When we consider the customs and understanding of a woman's *place* in ancient Israel, it is amazing that God used it to illustrate his point. If what you have is not the absolute best, you still have to work with what you've got. When dealing with fallen humanity, God has to deal with the worst, but he can turn it into something that is very good. As far as the way women were treated, we must ask ourselves: "What about Job's daughters?" The book of Job says: "And in all the land were no women found so fair as the daughters of Job: and their father gave them inheritance among their brethren" (Job 42:15). Many believe that the book of Job predates the Law of Moses during the time of the patriarchs (Abraham, Isaac, and Jacob). In studying Israel and God's relationship with them, we have to remember that there had been no final deliverance from sin in the Old Testament, and all they had was the Law and sacrifices that had to be offered again and again, but it was never enough due to the weakness of the flesh. Even within the Law, there was evidence of God's desire to treat women with equality. See Numbers 27:1–11 concerning God's laws of inheritance.

Jesus changed everything. He treated women with respect. Jesus had just directly revealed to the woman at the well that he was the Messiah when his disciples arrived. The Scripture says: "And upon this came his disciples, and marveled that he talked with the woman: yet no man said: What seekest thou? or, Why talkest thou with her?" (John 4:27). Even the Apostle Paul would write: "There is neither Jew nor Greek, there is neither bond nor free, there is neither male nor female: for ye are all one in Christ Jesus" (Galatians 3:28). Paul also had a lot to say about the Law and Jewish ritual as the apostle to the Gentiles, and he urges new believers: "Stand fast in the liberty wherewith Christ had made us free, and be not entangled again with the yoke of bondage" (Galatians 4:1).

Even with the Law of Moses, the weakness of the flesh was a formidable barrier that none could get over or around, and if one were to attempt to keep the law, he or she would have to have knowledge of all the law. Paul wrote: "For all have sinned, and come short of the glory of God" (Romans 3:23). God is completely pure and holy. Our sin must be dealt with before we can approach him. God illustrated this point in the desert of Sinai:

> And the Lord said unto Moses, Go unto the people, and sanctify them to day and to morrow, and let them wash their clothes, and be ready against the third day: for the third day the Lord will come down in the sight of all the people upon Mount Sinai.
>
> Exodus 19:10–11

Before they could witness the coming glory of God, both they and their garments must be cleansed and sanctified, and then they had to wait until the third day. There are no coincidences with God. When he uses a number, and especially when it is combined with a day, we had better pay attention. All the cleaning in the world could not really prepare them to meet their God, but God is clearly pointing to future redemption from the Law even before they would receive it, and they have to wait until the third day, also pointing to redemption through the power of the resurrection. Many are excited about Bible codes, but they overlook the obvious revelations of God that touch eternity while attempting to discover something about the future that is hidden in Scripture. The devil is trying to distract the bride! There has been something in Scripture that has been hidden from most church members for centuries. For the most part, theologians have ignored it. It's time we realized that the future is in God's hands. We simply need to prepare for Christ's return by loving one another while trusting God.

Man is not evolving into some higher life form; he is falling farther and farther away in his pride. The fall of man in the Garden of Eden had cost humanity their relationship with God, and God desires to restore the relationship. The only way to accomplish this is through a covenant agreement that depends completely on God. God desired a relationship with Israel, but he knew it would fail from the very beginning. We see the prideful people, even before they knew the Law, telling Moses that they will do all that the Lord says. They did not say by God's grace or with his help they would do his will. Instead, when Moses told them about God's plans, they said: "All that the Lord hath spoken, we will do" (Exodus 19:8b). Later, after having the Law read to them, they said: "All that the Lord hath said will we do, and be obedient" (Exodus 24:7b). This was an arrogant boast. God knew this and had given them the Law to allow them to see their sin. They needed the Law written in their hearts not on tablets of stone, but until they could come to this realization, they needed a schoolmaster. Paul would later write: "Wherefore the law was our schoolmaster to bring us unto Christ, that we might be justified by faith" (Galatians 3:24).

This attitude of pride is still keeping people from the God who loves them and has offered his only begotten Son to die in their place, as people either ignore God or try to appease him through their own efforts. To me, this is what makes grace so amazing! God desires a relationship with people who deny his existence, who take his name in vain, who rebel against his sovereignty, and who insist on doing things their own way. He loves people who pervert his Word and persecute his people, and he offers them redemption. Contrary to what some are preaching, he loves women who have had abortions, and he loves homosexuals. He loves drug dealers, murderers, and he even loves liars. God hates sin. He hates the awful things that people do, but God loves people. The relationship he desires to have with them is like a marriage relationship, but it has already been pointed out that God will not force this marriage on anyone. It is like becoming an adopted child of God who cannot lose his inheritance, but as God offers this adoption, he will not adopt anyone without their consent. But God's offer is soon to expire.

"The Lord looked down from heaven upon the children of men, to see if there were any that did understand, and seek God. They are all gone aside, they are all together become filthy; there is none that doeth good, no, not one" (Psalm 14:2–3).

God had told Noah that his Spirit would not always strive with man in Genesis 6:3, and then the flood began. He has told us that judgment is coming, and people still ignore all the warnings. We need God's forgiveness! Alfred Edersheim wrote: "…marriage conveyed to the Jews much higher thoughts than merely those of festivity and merriment. The pious fasted before it, confessing their sins. It was regarded almost as a sacrament. Entrance into the married state was thought to carry forgiveness of sins."[40] God is calling the world to the marriage feast of the Lamb. When you consider the meaning of marriage to the people that the Scriptures were written to, you must conclude that God has planned something wonderful for those who will trust in him and metaphorically become his bride.

Marriage is a covenant, and God desires a covenant relationship with his people. Marriage involves mutual commitment, and so does a relationship with God. Marriage requires self sacrifice, and so does a relationship with God. God loves sinners, and as sinners, we must love one another. But, like a husband, we must also learn to dwell with one another *according to knowledge.* God forgives, and so must we. God has patience beyond our imagination, and we should practice patience also. If the goal is to become like Christ, we should start and continue to emulate him in all things by the power he provides in the Spirit. He did not condemn the woman at the well in Samaria or the woman taken in the very act of adultery. He loved them and ministered to their immediate needs. He had a servant's heart, washing the feet of the disciples, who had been so very self-centered that the lesson was absolutely necessary. Christ ultimately sacrificed himself, and so should we. His sacrifice was not a metaphor. It was as real as it gets! And so was the resurrection.

God desires a relationship in which there is complete devotion and absolute fidelity. Raymond Ortlund said: "Yahweh's jealousy for his wife Israel requires that she offer her devotion to no other lover, just as a man will share his wife with no other."[41] As God was dealing with Israel, he was teaching and preparing us for a new and special relationship that would be offered first to Israel and then to the whole world. We may follow the *thread* of Scripture that continually points to this relationship and God's desires for us, and as we do, we will find that this thread is pretty big. If you will honestly look at the Scripture trail, you may find that it is like a seven-lane highway leading to God. At the end of this book, I have included a table that provides a partial picture of this biblical *thread*. Referring to it, you may see the many times that God is described as jealous. Remember that God is not jealous in the sense that a man or a woman might be jealous. God is completely righteous, and his jealousy refers to his real concern for our welfare. Ortlund had a footnote in his book that said: "The sharpness of the description 'jealous' when applied to God suggests that there are two kinds of jealousy. In fallen man, jealousy can be selfish and irrational; in God, jealousy is pure love."[42]

It would be fairly easy to criticize Israel and Judah for their infidelity and to overlook the same within the church. Being judgmental in hindsight does not excuse the idolatry that exists within the blood-bought body of Christ today. Many people who claim to be Christians are running to and fro, seeking the thrill of the natural and the supernatural without concern for discovering their true identity in Christ. Just as the Jews sought a sign, many today do the same. When will we learn that location is not the key to experiencing God? God is everywhere, and he is the friend who sticks closer than a brother (See Proverbs 18:28). One need not make a trip to the holy land or any earthly shrine to meet with and experience God's presence. We don't need a picture that represents Christ hanging on the wall to bow before or even a cross or a crucifix hanging within our field of vision. Personal preference for a particular worship style may also become a type of idolatry. Jesus told the woman at the well that true worshipers must worship in spirit and in truth. This stands in clear contrast to the hypocrisy of the priests, Levites, Pharisees, Sadducees, and scribes during Christ's days on earth. These people were going through the motions and trying to appear to be religious, seeking the approval of men, but they were not really seeking God with their whole heart. They were so dedicated to ritual cleanness that they overlooked true repentance because they did not think they were sinners. God desires a people that will be honest with themselves and honest with him. God desires a real relationship, but in a day of reality TV, it is becoming more and more difficult to discern what is real and what is play acting or hypocrisy.

God desires a people that are not selfish with their time, talents, or their property. He desires a people that are willing to give out of a pure heart to support his missions and ministry and for the care of those who are in need. God desires a people who will openly witness to the relationship that they have with him without shame, standing for him. Above all, God desires a people who will be Jesus to the world through the indwelling Holy Spirit and share his love with whosoever will come to him freely. God desires a compassionate people with whom he may have companionship, not because he needs us, but because we need him.

So, what is this relationship that God desires? It should be easily seen in the homes of believers everywhere, but in modern society, Christians are divorcing more than nonbelievers. Gary Thomas points out, "According to pollster George Barna, self-described 'born-again' Christians have a higher rate of divorce than nonbelievers (Twenty-seven percent to twenty-three percent)."[43] Like it or not, all believers are witnesses. They are either good witnesses, or they are bad ones, but they are all witnesses. The devil is working overtime trying to destroy the homes of believers, and becoming aware of the threat is a starting point from which we may move forward. For many, it is too late to reclaim or renew their vows. The big problem is that they did not fully understand the vows they originally made, but this is no excuse. Adam and Eve did not fully understand the result of their disobedience, but they had to live and die with those results. God desires a perfect relationship involving total commitment, but he knows the weakness of the human flesh and provides strength for every trial if we will remember to rely on him and his strength during times of difficulty.

Actually, we need to learn to rely on him all the time. But since we are not God, and never will be, human frailty is going to produce situations where divorce is an option.

If God can divorce Israel, why can't a man divorce his wife or a wife divorce her husband and still be free to continue their lives and even marry again? Be careful with your answer in this question and don't immediately jump to a proof text to support your decision. The Bible gives examples of acceptable grounds for divorce. Jesus pointed out adultery, and he knew about these grounds on a first-hand basis because Israel had been adulterous in their relationship with God. Paul wrote: "But if the unbelieving depart, let him depart. A brother or a sister is not under bondage in such cases: but God hath called us to peace" (I Corinthians 7:15). Based on this scripture, desertion seems to be another ground for divorce and should allow for remarriage. But were Jesus or Paul trying to give us a comprehensive listing of all situations where divorce is acceptable, or were they trying to convey a greater truth? Since Jesus described lust as adultery in the Sermon on the Mount, what would actually constitute adultery making it grounds for divorce? Where does repentance come into the picture? If one asks forgiveness of both God and men and turns from the sin, striving not to repeat it again, does not freedom come with repentance? Men and women find themselves looking for a way out of their marriage because they are unhappy or bored with the relationship, and at times, they don't even seem to have a real relationship. God does not do this! God is constantly working with an unwilling and many times seemingly absent and apathetic partner, trying to improve the relationship, but as we have already seen in Isaiah and Jeremiah, there is a limit to what God will put up with.

What about a situation with a man who beats and continually abuses his wife? Should she be advised to stay and hope he changes or mellows over the years? Some have been given this advice! How foolish! I don't care how religious a man claims to be or tries to appear, if he is abusing his wife or children, according to 1 John, he is a liar. In Hebrew society, this would have been the rabbinical advice based upon their treatment of women and the way they considered them property. But we are not living in those days anymore. Praise God! Sadly, however, it has been the advice of well meaning ministers who thought they were applying the message of the Bible. Whoever is the abusive partner in a marriage relationship has already broken their vows, and there is no point in remaining in an abusive marriage that might produce permanent injury or even death. The New Testament does not list incest as a reason for divorce, but do you think that God would want a man or a woman to stay in a marriage where a son or daughter were being continually molested? A little common sense is needed. Paul deals with incest, though not by name, in 1 Corinthians 5:1–5, but instead of divorce, the perpetrator of this deed is to be cast out of the church and delivered to Satan for the good of the church and for his own good. This would serve as a warning of coming judgment to the rest of the body.

Divorce, in the case of spousal abuse or incest, might also be seen as a revelation of God's judgment.

God doesn't overlook sin. He has never tried to ignore it, hoping that it would just go away. I don't believe that he expects us to ignore sin, either. If sin is in our own lives, he expects us to confess it and turn from it. Jesus told the woman taken in adultery to go and sin no more. Scripture does not specifically mention addiction to pornography or drugs, but the believers are cautioned not to allow anything to gain control of their lives. Sins of addiction are called sickness today, but no germ or virus has ever been identified that causes these so-called diseases. We need to learn to identify sin as sin, but we need to begin by looking in the mirror of our own soul. Paul asked: "Know ye not that we shall judge angels? How much more the things that pertain to this life?" (I Corinthians 6:3). Gary Thomas said: "I have a theory: Behind virtually every case of marital dissatisfaction lies unrepented sin."[44] Speaking of Christian brothers he met in Bible College who had been divorced before their conversions, Keener says: "Although most of the students I knew seemed to sympathize with them, these prospective ministers were told by certain professors that they may as well give up on their calling altogether, because this very conservative denomination would not license them."[45]

Excuse me, but it is not a denomination that calls someone to Christian service. It is God. This reminds me of the story of the two men who found themselves in prison. One, a Christian, who had been falsely accused and wrongly convicted of a crime, was divorced by his wife while he was in prison. The other, a lost man who was in prison for killing his wife, accepted Christ in prison. Several years later, they were both released and joined the same church, and both served there for several more years. The church found itself in need of deacons and considered the man who had killed his wife and was later saved, but it would not consider the falsely accused man because he had been divorced. Some churches accept repentant and reformed alcoholics, drug addicts, murderers, gang members, and thieves, but not someone who has been divorced, even if they were not at fault. The church even accepts unrepentant gossips and members who rob God by withholding their tithes. This sounds a bit hypocritical to me. Why is divorce considered separately?

What was Jesus talking about when he said that anyone who puts away his wife and marries commits adultery? Speaking of putting away one's wife as Jesus mentions in Matthew 19:9, Lamsa, who says that Jesus spoke Aramaic, says: "The Aramaic word 'shvikta' means 'an undivorced woman.' This should be understood to mean, 'a woman whose husband has not given her divorce papers.'"[46] He then says, "The Aramaic word for divorced is 'shrita,' which means the one on whom the sacred bond has loosened."[47] So, what Lamsa is saying is that Jesus was teaching about the Jews taking advantage of the laxity of the law, and "He (Jesus) only attacked those who married women who were not actually divorced by law."[48] If it were to prove to be correct, this would give a whole new meaning to Jesus' discourse on the topic of divorce that has been taken so literally by the church for centuries. Regardless of your interpretation of this verse or your understanding of the meaning, Jesus was not really dealing with the problem of divorce; he is answering a question put forth by the Pharisees and is dealing with the hardness of their hearts and their attempts to trap him into saying something that they could use against him. He clearly states that what God has joined together, man should not put asunder. What constitutes a marriage that God has truly "joined" together? Does God join together people who get drunk or drugged up and get married on a whim, waking up the next morning with someone they don't know beside them on the bed? Does God join together the devil's children in marriage? These Pharisees had put much more than marriage asunder, and he called them an adulterous and sinful generation in Mark 8:38. They were seeking a particular sign, but they never received the sign that they wanted. He certainly was not giving us a new law. He was simply explaining an old law. When he did put forth a new law, he identified it as such: "A new commandment I give unto you, That ye love one another; as I have loved you, that ye also love one another" (John 13:34). In dealing with people who have been divorced, this new commandment of Christ is seldom considered.

The legalism of the New Testament church does not glorify God any more than the legalism of the Pharisees did. Jesus also gave us the golden rule, but it has been set aside many times in the name of righteousness. What is righteous about condemning the innocent in a situation that they could do absolutely nothing to prevent? I can tell you from personal experience that if your wife chooses to leave you for another man, there is nothing that you can do to prevent it but pray, and sometimes God says, "No." God did not prevent Israel from forsaking him, but when she did, he divorced her, but he had a plan to recover the relationship through the blood of his Son.

Growing up in the church, I remember the testimonies of drug addicts, atheists, thieves, gang members, and murderers as they related their deliverance to the youth group or the church, and everyone was amazed at the power of God to forgive and to save, but I can't recall a single testimony from anyone that God had strengthened or that the church had supported through a divorce. As a young man, I concluded that this particular sin must be unforgivable. Then it happened to me, and I thought my ministry was over, and a lot of people that I know encouraged me to believe that it was over. But God was not through with me! And if you have been divorced, let me assure you that God is not finished with you, either. Although God uses marriage as a picture of the relationship that he desires to have with you, nothing, not even the failure of your marriage to your earthly spouse, can sever the tie that binds you to God.

A case study in Rubel Shelly's book tells of a battered wife. Shelly writes:

> He hit her seven-year-old daughter hard enough last week that he ruptured her left eardrum. Ellen was at her parents' home when she called the preacher from their little church. He encouraged her to come home, give her husband another chance, and pray real hard for things to work out for them.[49]
>
> Shelly, 10

Shelly then says: "Divorce is not a good thing. But is it worse than spousal abuse?" [50]

A few years ago, as I sat in my office at the church, I received a phone call from a woman who would not identify herself. She said she had married a man with a teenage son, and her husband had suggested that she keep his son sexually satisfied to keep him at home and out of trouble. Although she claimed to be a Christian, she had given in to this suggestion, and now the teenager would not leave her alone. As she related her story, I told her that what she was doing was wrong in the sight of God and the law, and I suggested that she get counseling as soon as possible. I assured her that God still loved her and that he could help her out of this mess. She was guilty of being obedient to her husband and sexually abusing a minor, but she wanted to blame her husband and the boy. If I had known her identity, I would have been required by law to report the abuse of a minor child, and at that time, I didn't even have caller ID. People have a way of digging holes for themselves from which there seems to be no way of escape. She could have said no, but she didn't, and now she felt trapped. Sin always takes you further than you want to go. What would you have told her? God offers forgiveness, but he requires repentance, and he is not obligated to shield us from the consequences of sin.

Do you believe yet that the devil is trying to destroy traditional marriage? There are so many stories of spousal abuse, child abuse, and sexual immorality. The devil is very busy, but he can't be blamed for all the sin. The devil doesn't make a person sin, he simply entices. People are the ones who make the poor choices. They choose to enjoy the moment without considering the consequences. Meanwhile, God still desires to have a personal relationship with humanity, but too many only seek his will after they have messed up so badly that there seems to be no other way. Amazingly, God will allow anyone to fall this far, if it will cause them to call on him. Consider the well known story of the prodigal son. He had lost everything before he "came to himself" and realized that his father's servants weren't starving; so, he decided to go back to his father's house and ask for a job. Along the way he planned his apology, but his father saw him and ran to meet him, accepting him back as a son, not as a servant.

God simply wants his family to come home! He has a big party planned, and he has set the date, but we aren't told exactly when it will be. We are simply told to be ready. How are we preparing? Are we doing what Jesus told us to do? Are we loving one another as he loved us? I observe the legalism that is applied without concern for mercy within many churches and denominations, and I don't see a lot of love. Jesus told the Pharisees: "But if ye had known what this meaneth, I will have mercy, and not sacrifice, ye would not have condemned the guiltless" (Matthew 12:7). Have we ever condemned the guiltless? Christ was defending his disciples in this passage of scripture because the Pharisees had accused them of breaking Sabbath rules. Jesus didn't sound very happy about their condemning attitudes. How do you think Christ feels about the judgmental and condemning attitudes of church members that he has bled and died to redeem? Discipline is needed in the church, but it must be applied in a spirit of love and humility.

God is dealing with an imperfect people in an imperfect world, trying to establish a perfect church, and he is trying to reveal a perfect truth through a metaphor about an imperfect human relationship to illustrate the perfect relationship that he desires to have with his people. God uses imperfect people because there are no perfect people. Only God is perfect. Is the church a country club for saints, or is it a rehabilitation center for sinners? Actually, it is neither. It is the bride of Christ being adorned and perfected by God for his purposes. It is the body of Christ created to minister to a sin-damaged world. Church discipline is necessary, but we should be very careful in how it is applied. We don't want to be the cause of anyone's stumbling. We hear Jesus in Luke 13:1–2: "Then said he to the disciples, 'It is impossible but that offences will come: but woe unto him, through whom they come! It were better for him that a millstone be hanged around his neck, and he be cast into the sea, than that he should offend one of these little ones.'"

God desires a special relationship with a people that he has purchased with the blood of Christ. Just as Hosea had to buy his wife back, God has purchased us. Just as Boaz redeemed Naomi and Ruth, God has redeemed those who believe. He has taken responsibility for us and promises to preserve, protect, and provide for us, but most of all, he has called us to be his companion and friend. In John 15:15, Jesus told his disciples that he no longer called them servants but friends. Are we acting like friends of God or friends of the world? Like adopted children, God wants us to grow and learn to be productive in his family and in the world. If you have been divorced, I know that God still has plans for you, even if you were the guilty party. Anyone who admits their sin and turns from it can be forgiven. He can even teach you something from the terrible experience. Paul, who had been complicit in the murder of Stephen, wrote: "And we know that all things work together for good to them that love God, to them who are the called according to his purpose" (Romans 8:28). A few verses later he would ask: "Who shall separate us from the love of Christ?" (Romans 8:35a). Paul said that *all* things work together for good. He didn't say only good things or good experiences work for our good. Satan may intend something for evil as a person falls into his trap, but God can turn it against him and use it for his glory through the forgiven and empowered life of a believer who will not fall into the same trap again and who now has the insight from experience to warn others of the dangers of sin or even to minister to the fallen. After all, *you have been there.*

THE UNFAITHFUL
WIFE OF GOD

In the prophets, Israel is described as being a harlot and totally unfaithful to the One who provides for and cares for her. Isaiah says:

> For thy maker is thine husband; the Lord of Hosts is his name; and thy Redeemer the Holy One of Israel; the God of the whole earth shall he be called. For the Lord hath called thee as a woman forsaken and grieved in spirit, and a wife of youth, when thou wast refused, saith the Lord.
>
> Isaiah 54:5–6

Jeremiah said: "Surely as a wife treacherously departs from her husband, so have ye dealt treacherously with me, O house of Israel, saith the Lord" (Jeremiah 3:20). Describing Jerusalem, Ezekiel 16:15 says: "But thou didst trust in thine own beauty, and playedst the harlot because of thy renown, and pouredst out thy fornications on every one that passed by; his it was." Hosea

4:15 says: "Though thou, Israel, play the harlot, yet let not Judah offend; and come not ye to Gilgal, neither go ye up to Bethaven, nor swear, the Lord liveth."

This is the same kind of language used to describe the city of Nineveh by Nahum as he spoke of its certain destruction by God. Nahum said of Nineveh: "Because of the multitude of the whoredoms of the wellfavoured harlot, the mistress of witchcrafts, that selleth nations through her whoredoms, and families through her witchcrafts" (Nahum 3:4). It is abundantly clear that God equates idolatry with harlotry and whoredom since he expects fidelity from his people just as a husband expects the same from his wife. God equates witchcraft with rebellion. Samuel told King Saul: "For rebellion is as the sin of witchcraft, and stubbornness is as iniquity and idolatry. Because thou hast rejected the word of the Lord, he hath also rejected thee from being king" (I Samuel 15:23)

In reference to Jeremiah 2:35–37, John Walvoord says:

> After a stinging indictment declaring that Israel was guilty of spiritual harlotry, God declared his purpose to judge her, 'But I will pass judgment on you because you say, I have not sinned (v. 35). God informed her that though she would turn away from Egypt as well as Assyria, You will also leave that place with your hands on your head, for the Lord has rejected those you trust; you will not be helped by them (v. 37).[51]
>
> Walvoord, 122

Walvoord also spoke of the "unfaithfulness" of Judah as seen in Jeremiah 3:11–18, but he does not mention the metaphorical husband and wife relationship. He calls Israel and Judah "she" or "her," but that is as far as he goes. I don't think he is avoiding the subject; he simply doesn't see it as important to prophecy.

It is also interesting that Walvoord skips from Jeremiah 2:35–37 to Jeremiah 3: 11–18, bypassing the divorce of Israel by God that is found in Jeremiah 3:8–9. Since this was a metaphorical prophecy about the destruction of Israel and he left it out, it makes one wonder. Earlier in his book, Walvoord mentioned the heretical school in Alexandria, Egypt that translated everything in the Bible as allegorical or non-literal in the third century, and he said that they subverted all the major doctrines of the faith, but when faced with a verse that could not possibly be taken literally, he simply skips it in his book. Toward the middle of Walvoord's book, as he examined Hosea, he said: "Throughout the book the marriage relation between Hosea and his adulterous wife Gomer provided the unifying thread through the prophecies of Hosea and typically represented the relationship of Yahweh and the twelve tribes of Israel viewed as an adulterous wife."[52]

God truly loves Israel, but his love is not always returned. In order for the people to understand his pain, he calls Hosea to do something that he asked no other prophet to do. Hosea was to marry Gomer, who was a whore. Many have had great difficulty with this passage and have tried to say that she became a harlot after Hosea took her to be his wife, but scripturally, this argument does not hold water. Were the Hebrew people that God delivered out of Egypt pure, chaste, and holy? No. At the first opportunity they made a golden calf and worshiped it as the god that had delivered them out of bondage. Aaron actually shaped the idol, and when he was confronted by Moses, he said: "And I said unto them, whosoever hath any gold, let them break it off. So they gave it me: then I cast it into the fire, and there came out this calf" (Exodus 32:24). This was Aaron! Three thousand men were killed as a result of this sin. We may not always like what God says, but we must remember that he is God, and he is always right. Hosea was to marry Gomer so that God's people and Hosea would understand what God was going through in dealing with Israel and Judah. Do you think that Hosea got a glimpse or a taste of the agony that God's people had put him through? He certainly gained an understanding through experience, but he was only dealing with one woman while God was struggling with a whole nation of harlots.

Did God want his prophets to record all of this in Scripture so that we could be judgmental and condemn Israel's ignorance, feeling superior in our informed relationship with Christ? No! We definitely have been blessed with greater revelation, but that does not make us superior. It makes us responsible to observe, learn, and respond to God's warnings. We should not make the same mistakes, but we do. We still doubt, murmur, and complain. God's Word is misinterpreted and misapplied. We hear the proclamations of the prophets concerning Israel as the unfaithful wife and think that perhaps if we had been there, we wouldn't have made the same mistake. We need to wake up and smell the coffee or the incense, or something!

Israel was put away or divorced by God because of their idolatry, their alliances, their spiritual promiscuity, and their wandering hearts. They are described as harlots. What is a harlot, or a whore, or a prostitute? This is someone who sells sexual favors and companionship for money, and it may be seen in many forms. All prostitutes are not street walkers. If women or men set their sights on marrying for money, isn't this a form of prostitution? If we join a church because it is good for business, isn't this also prostitution? Anything that we do for personal gain that is in any way dishonest, deceptive, or immoral could also fit the description, because we would be selling ourselves for money, and anything upon which we place a higher value or a higher priority than our relationship with the one true God becomes our personal idol.

Prostitution comes in many forms. But Israel was classified as a harlot who refused her pay. She was simply committing whoredom because she enjoyed it. Many people today could be placed in this category. It's all about the thrill of the moment. Back in the sixties, their battle cry was: if it feels good, do it. But should we base our lives on something as fickle and fleeting as feelings, or should we look for a rock foundation like the unchanging Word of God? Wow! Talk about a no-brainer! Many, however, within religious circles are actually more inclined to trust their feelings than they are to trust and apply God's Word. Perhaps this is due to ignorance of God's Word or because it requires some effort, and we are a society that enjoys convenience. This is even used to circumvent the Bible, as people say that they feel like something is the will of God for their lives, regardless of what God has already stated with perfect clarity. It doesn't matter what you may feel; God is not telling you to leave your wife or husband for someone else. Someone may be whispering in your ear, but it isn't God.

False teachers abound in the world today, and Scripture warns of the deception, but who has time to read the Bible? Paul wrote: "For the time will come when they will not endure sound doctrine; but after their own lusts shall they heap to themselves teachers, having itching ears; and they shall turn away their ears from the truth, and shall be turned to fables" (II Timothy 4:3–4). If you don't study God's Word for yourself, and you just follow the teachings of some charismatic leader, you may find yourself "drinking the Kool-aid" or standing at God's throne of judgment, hearing the words: "Depart from me. I never knew you."

The unfaithful wife of God was just trying to fit in to her surroundings and be hospitable to her neighbors. She was simply trying to identify with those around her and prevent conflict. Has the church ever done this? How much do we have to compromise in order to have our witness weakened? But we should be very careful in deciding what constitutes compromise. There is a lot of campaigning going on in the country today that passes as righteousness. God never told Israel to "straighten out" her neighbors. He simply said they were not to make any covenant with them. It is not our job to reform the country or the world. We couldn't do this if we wanted to. It is our job to love one another and love the lost. We are to pray for them, and we are to offer them the gospel in a kind and compassionate way. God's plan is to change the world one person at a time from the inside out. He doesn't force people into the kingdom, and he doesn't impose his rules on the devil's children. But we must be careful what we do in order to fit in to society and accommodate the world. The church is to be in the world but not of the world!

I have heard a few cynical people at weddings talking about the couple's chances for longevity in their relationship. They say, "It will never last," or "I give it a few months." What about Israel's marriage to God? Was there ever any hope for this marriage? Raymond Ortlund wrote: "It is significant that the clearest marital images early in the story of the covenanted people are Israel's whoredom and Yahweh's jealousy in return. From the beginning, the marriage was strained. That tension will break out into open conflict in the prophetic literature."[53] What was the weakness in the relationship with Israel? We have already established that God is not now nor has he ever been the problem. Israel was the problem. Sin was and is the problem.

People are simply incapable of having a sustained relationship with God without God's help. Paul wrote in his letter to the church at Rome: "So then they that are in the flesh cannot please God" (Romans 8:8). But he said of the church: "But ye are not in the flesh, but in the Spirit, if so be that the Spirit of God dwell in you. Now if any man have not the Spirit of Christ, he is none of his" (Romans 8:9). The Old Testament people of God had an external relationship with a set of rules to live by that depended completely upon their capacity to remain in line with God's will by obeying his Law. Their situation was hopeless based upon Paul's words in Romans 8, but they were extremely blessed in that they were given great revelation; however, they remained under a curse that they could not escape. In Galatians 3:10, Paul illustrates this very point: "For as many as are of the works of the law are under the curse: for it is written, cursed is every one that continueth not in all things which are written in the book of the law to do them." Paul would then speak of Christ's redeeming us from the curse of the law. If the law holds nothing but condemnation and curse, why do so many people seem to still desire subjection to it? I think that it is because self-righteousness demands legality. If you want a strained relationship with God, just develop a self-righteous attitude. Observe and point out all the faults of others and deny that you have any faults because of your religious activities or your pious lifestyle. The spirit of the Pharisees is alive and well today in the church within too many people's hearts.

Referring to the law as written in Deuteronomy 24:1–4, Ortlund says:

> How feebly the people grasped the significance of their compromises with the Baals. To them, it was inconsequential; to Yahweh, it was inexcusable. Without realizing it, Judah had created an impossible situation, placing herself beyond redemption—at least within the provisions of the law.[54]

Ortlund, 91

The law clearly stated that if a man put his wife away and she married another, that man could not take her back for himself even if the new husband were to die. A little later in his book, Ortlund would say: "Having wrecked their marriage with Yahweh and gone off to many others, the people may not expect restoration to their first husband."[55] Ortlund then adds: "There is no going back for Jeremiah's generation."[56] The key here is "Jeremiah's generation," the people who had actually committed harlotry with the Baals, would not be forgiven, but their descendants would find new opportunity in God's plan of eternal redemption through Jesus Christ.

What were the acts of unfaithfulness that caused God to divorce Israel? Going back to God's deliverance from Egypt, the people made solemn promise to the Lord that they would completely obey his Law and serve only him. They promised to do all that God said in Exodus 24:3, but just before they said this, God said what he would do for them, and he spoke of the land he would give them. God said of the people they would encounter in the land: "Thou shalt make no covenant with them, or with their gods. They shall not dwell in thy land, lest they make thee sin against me, for if thou serve their gods, it will surely be a snare unto thee" (Exodus 23:32–33). God knew as he spoke these words that they would do exactly what he had told them not to do. God is never surprised at any actions we take, any thoughts that we have, or any inaction on our part, and he loves us anyway. This, again, is why grace is so amazing. Israel broke their vows and forsook their God, and they did it with great fervor. Isaiah, Jeremiah,

Ezekiel, Hosea, and Micah all referred to the people as harlots for worshiping false gods. Isaiah and Jeremiah both speak of divorce. Ortlund talks about his proposals that he says are grounded in exegesis and says:

> … the bond between Yahweh and Israel is marital in nature. In the Pentateuch and historical books, the indicators of this deeper theological substructure underlying the text are found in the references to Israel's whoredom in sharing her relationship with other gods and in Yahweh's jealousy for her.[57]

Ortlund, 26

In Hosea's time the kingdom was divided with Israel in the north and Judah in the south. Israel was Hosea's topic, and he warned Judah with the judgment he proclaimed against Israel. Julia O'Brien writes: "Hosea quickly establishes the marriage metaphor. God tells the prophet to take an unfaithful woman not because he loves her or in order to turn her life around but rather to make a point: Israel, like a woman, has been unfaithful."[58] O'Brien also says: "The vocabulary used for Gomer/Israel's unfaithfulness is sexually loaded. She is a 'harlot' (RSV), or a 'whore' (NRSV), or an 'adulteress' (NIV)."[59] She will go on to say that the Hebrew word literally denotes a prostitute. God is not trying to be abusive to women in these instances; he is merely providing an example of the unfaithfulness of his people who had sworn to do all that the Lord had said. Feminist writers have looked at Hosea and declared parts of it pornographic. Of course it should be noted that these women have entered into the study of God's Word with a personal agenda. O'Brien also says:

> The acceptance of this feminist insight has given birth to the catchy damning label "pornoprophetics." Since its appearance in Athalaya Brenner's comparison of the book of Jeremiah with *The Story of O,* a French pornographic novel, the label has become a part of the standard vocabulary by which feminists describe the sexualized violence against women that characterizes the prophetic materials. [60]
>
> O'Brien, 35

It is very difficult to be politically correct when you are trying to present the possibility of redemption to a nation of whores, and God and his prophets did not mince words. This was a very serious problem that cost Israel the kingdom. God was not interested in being politically correct or gender correct. He was and is making a point that he expects loyalty, and he expects his people to keep their promises. He wanted them to find everlasting joy and everlasting truth in the person of Jesus Christ, whom he would send to pay the penalty for all the sins that are mentioned by the prophets.

Every declaration of judgment from the mouths or pens of the prophets is a call to repentance. I have discovered over the years that when a person is confronted with the reality of his own sin, he will either be convicted and repentant or will get angry. Observing the Pharisees, anger and hatred for Christ ate their souls like a cancer. Anger, hatred, and complete resentment will keep anyone from the kingdom. If you come into the study of God's Word with your own agenda, seeking proof texts for your position, you will probably find exactly what you are looking for, but it will not be God's message of perfect redemption and love. There are some pretty harsh words in the Bible, but taken in context and considering the historic environment of women in the Bible, I think that feminists should thank God that we don't live in those times anymore. Everything that God does is motivated by his love for us. He has provided a perfect salvation, and through his spirit he is preparing a bride for his Son. It's going to be a glorious wedding, and no one will want to keep their old name. Sorry! As believers, Christ is our identity right now, but when we see him in glory, it's going to be too wonderful for words.

Just as God has a plan to take a new bride and establish the church, he still has a plan for the restoration of the relationship with all Israel. As we examine the prophecies of the Old Testament, we discover the promises about the land that God has given them; and Isaiah, who like the other prophets, has some very condemning things to say, also has a picture of a very bright hope. Isaiah writes:

> For Zion's sake will I not hold my peace, and for Jerusalem's sake I will not rest, until the righteousness go forth as brightness, and the salvation thereof as a lamp that burneth. And the Gentiles shall see thy righteousness, and all the kings thy glory: and thou shalt be called by a new name, which the mouth of the Lord shall name. Thou shalt also be a crown of glory in the hand of the

Lord, and a royal diadem in the hand of thy God. Thou shalt no more be termed Forsaken; neither shall thy land be any more termed Desolate: but thou shalt be called Hepzibah, and thy land Beulah: for the Lord delighteth in thee, and thy land shall be called married. For as a young man marrieth a virgin, so shall thy sons marry thee: and as the bridegroom rejoiceth over the bride, so shall thy God rejoice over thee.

Isaiah 62:1–5

There are differing views as to what God is telling Israel in this passage. Some think it refers to the forming of the church because of the mention of the bride and bridegroom. Some think it refers to Israel's restoration during the millennial reign of Christ, and some think it refers to heaven and our eternal home, and there are songs about Beulah land that seem to be synonymous with our home in heaven. God's promises to Israel were about the land, and this prophecy calls the land married, not the people. The word *Hepzibah* means "my delight is in her," and *Beulah* means "married." There is no doubt that the term "married" could be and has been applied to the church as well as Israel, but Isaiah is speaking to Israel. Their land will be called Beulah because of the new and special relationship that God is going to create with her in the future, and he will delight in her. When we consider the context of the chapters surrounding this passage, I have to hold to the idea that this is about the restored Jerusalem during Christ's millennial reign. But why the mention of the land being married? God did not promise Israel heaven, because through the law, there was no way of eternal redemption. There was only condemnation as a breaker of the law, but in Christ, the law is fulfilled, and the final sacrifice is offered forever. However, Israel did not understand or receive her Messiah when he came to them. God, who cannot lie, will keep his promises to Israel, and the land will be called married, not the people. This is a big difference! The bride of Christ received no promises about the land, but God promised the church an eternal relationship and a home with God.

Is the bride of Christ fully committed and faithful to God? It does not always appear to be. Are Christian husbands always true and faithful to their wives? Okay, there is such a thing as a dumb question. Unfaithfulness comes in many forms. In the Sermon on the Mount, Jesus said: "Ye have heard that it was said by them of old time, Thou Shalt Not Commit Adultery: But I say unto you, That whosoever looketh on a woman to lust after her hath already committed adultery with her in his heart" (Matthew 5:27–28). In Jesus' day, there were no pornographic magazines or movies. There were no phone sex lines or Internet porn sites. But people had imaginations. Before the flood, it was observed: "And God saw that the wickedness of man was great in the earth, and that every imagination of the thoughts of his heart was only evil continually" (Genesis 6:5). Nothing has changed, but that imagination has devised more ways to indulge in sin and profit financially from it while using and abusing men, women, and children. Remember that Paul warned Timothy that the love of money is the root of all evil in I Timothy 6:10. Is your imagination submitted to the authority of Christ? To whom or what are you submitting yourself? Just as a man should keep his earthly marriage pure and remain faithful to his wife in all things, believers should remain true and faithful to God. We should be careful what we put before our eyes, what we listen to, and what we think about. This can be a very difficult struggle, but it is a war that has to be fought one battle at a time. We are not alone in these battles. "And the Lord shall deliver me from every evil work, and will preserve me unto his heavenly kingdom: to who be glory for ever and ever. Amen" (II Timothy 4:18).

GOD'S DIVORCE CASE

According to the policy of many churches and denominations, God the Father would not be qualified to be a pastor, because he has been divorced. According to both Isaiah and Jeremiah, God divorced Israel. But we must look at the grounds for God's divorce, and we must remember that it is impossible for God to sin or lie. I am not trying to justify divorce, but God was well within his rights in divorcing Israel, and he did not sin. Actually, he had to do it. Their sin of idolatry was like a cancer, and it had to be removed. No man or woman can claim absolute innocence in a divorce. We all make mistakes, but God had done nothing but good for Israel, and all his attempts to demonstrate his love and to demand fidelity were ignored. In Jeremiah 3:8, God gave Israel a bill of divorce because of her adultery. In Isaiah 50:1, God asks where the bill of divorcement is for Israel's mother and says that it is for their transgressions that she is put away. In both of these passages of scripture, all hope is not lost. God has a plan for redemption!

When searching for sources that discuss divorce in the Bible, they are somewhat limited, unless you want to wade through a pile of feminist literature. As previously stated, the *Dictionary of Biblical Imagery* does not even include divorce or putting away, and John Walvoord simply skipped over God's divorce of Israel in his book about prophecy. Malachi 2:16 says: "For the Lord God of Israel saith that he hateth putting away: for one covereth violence with his garment, saith the Lord of hosts: therefore take heed to your spirit, that ye deal not treacherously." Some modern versions translate this as "God hates divorce" instead of "putting away." George M. Lamsa would say that this is totally different from divorce but rather signifies an illegal separation that does not take into account the rights of the wife that is being put away, and just kicking her out of the house without proper divorce papers would be to send her into homelessness with no remedy apart from returning to her family in disgrace. Anyone who has been through a divorce, no matter how they proclaim their relief, truly hates that it happened, and God had divorced Israel, so he understands the agony involved. In II Peter 3:9, the Bible says that God is longsuffering and not willing that any should perish, but Israel's idolatry forced his hand, and the divorce was a judgment of the nation's sins. God will not overlook sin forever.

What about God's case for divorce? He had delivered Israel from bondage. He had led her through the wilderness and fed her with bread from heaven. He had called water out of a rock in the desert and supplied all her needs. He had comforted her and treated her with the utmost kindness. He deserved loyalty and trust, but he received rejection and infidelity. He wasn't surprised by the actions of his called out people. In fact, he expected it and had a plan in place to redeem them from the foundation of the world. God knew what was going to happen from the beginning, and I can't help but wonder why he even created us, but he answers that question in John 3:16. Everything that God does is motivated by love.

He began by instituting marriage, and the lessons began. With this marriage of Adam and Eve, he was demonstrating the relationship that he desires to have with all of his creation. But it is a creation that had to be given free will. God could have made robots to serve him, but he wanted his love returned just as a husband or wife desires a return of their love. He desired companionship, but he did not want a group of yes men following him around and agreeing with everything he said against their will. It is a relationship that he desires, not a religion, and certainly not empty ritual.

If, as the modern translations say, God hates divorce, how does he feel about those who exclude and look down on those who have been divorced? Is there life after divorce? Is it the unforgivable and eternal sin? In God's divorce case, he immediately speaks of a new marriage that he has planned. Again, considering the foreknowledge of God, he knew the divorce would be necessary, and he knew he would marry again. Why did he go through all this? If we consider that all of God's revelation is progressive, it makes perfect sense. The Hebrew people were never ready for anything that God wanted to give to them, and this pretty much describes the plight of all mankind. Nobody is ready to meet God, and serving him is not a natural choice. God's divorce case is a revelation of judgment on those who reject his love, rule, and authority. Marriage, as a metaphor, reveals the relationship desired by God, and the divorce demonstrates the severity of judgment of all those who reject the bridegroom. The first divorce is when Adam and Eve deserted God and chose to heed the words of the serpent rather than obeying God, and a second picture of divorce may be seen in Abraham's sending Hagar and Ishmael away to please Sarah.

Joseph's brothers rejected him and sold him into slavery because they weren't ready for him to rule over them. The people rejected Moses, asking in Exodus 2:14: "Who made thee a prince and a judge over us?" According to Jesus, they rejected and killed the prophets that God sent, and they ultimately cried out for the death of Christ and rejected his rule over them as well. So, who rejected and deserted whom, and who divorced whom? Israel was unfaithful, and she abandoned God to worship idols. The two biblical grounds for divorce both came into play. In the New Testament, infidelity and abandonment by a non-believer are both recognized as grounds for a divorce.

God's divorce was an absolute necessity! He could not allow things to continue as they were. Israel's sin was a result of their unbelief. If they had believed God, they would have obeyed his warnings. God had warned:

> Take heed to yourselves, that ye be not deceived, and ye turn aside, and serve other gods, and worship them; And then the Lord's wrath be kindled

against you, and he shut up the heaven, that there be no rain, and that the land yield not her fruit; and lest ye perish quickly from off the good land which the Lord giveth you.

Deuteronomy 11:16–17

God's warning about the consequences of idolatry involves the withholding of his blessing on the land and possible starvation of the people due to drought and famine. God invented tough love! All the promises to Israel involved the land and their descendants. The world is deceived in many ways. People take God for granted. They seem to think that if there is a God, he will just let things continue as they are. They are deceived into thinking that they are responsible for their own existence and that humanity can ultimately find a way to work things out. The apostle Paul wrote: "Be not deceived; God is not mocked: for whatsoever a man soweth, that shall he also reap" (Galatians 6:7). R. G. Lee's sermon *Payday Someday* still rings true. God will not overlook sin forever, and a payday is on the way. Jeremiah said: "And I saw, when for all the causes whereby backsliding Israel committed adultery I had put her away, and given her a bill of divorce; yet her treacherous sister Judah feared not, but went and played the harlot also" (Jeremiah 3:8). God is serious about dealing with the sin that separates us from him. The clock of time is ticking and will soon grind to a halt. God has judged in the past, and he will do so again in the near future, but in the meanwhile, he calls all people everywhere to believe and stop following their own path (repent) and to follow Jesus Christ.

I see God's divorce as a call to repentance and faith. God was setting everything in place in preparation for the coming Messiah. People, especially theologians, seem to think that they understand God and how he works and what he likes and dislikes. Israel thought they understood, but the Messiah they got was not the Messiah they were looking for or expecting. They had heard all the prophecies and were convinced that Messiah would put all their enemies under their feet and restore David's kingdom. Jesus, however, said they should love their enemies. This wasn't the message they expected, and it certainly wasn't the message that they wanted. God was progressively revealing his plan to solve the problem of sin and rebellion for all people for all eternity, but other people and eternity were not high on their priority list. They were more interested in themselves and their nation, and for the most part, they were interested in the here and now. This sounds like the world today. Not much has changed.

Another great divorce is coming! God is going to finally deal with the problem of sin, suffering, disease, death, and the devil. Just as he put away a sinful nation to whom he had offered life, progeny, and prosperity in the Promised Land, he will put away death and the grave. Just as God flooded the entire world and started over with eight people, he will begin anew, but this time, there will be no deception and no deceiver to thwart his plan. Not only is another divorce on the way, but a wedding is also planned and everyone is invited, but not everyone will respond to the invitation.

Jesus offered two different parables that especially illustrate this point. They are the parable of the king's wedding feast for his son and the parable of the ten virgins. The parable of the king's wedding feast is in Matthew 25:1–13, and it pictures the ones invited, Israel, rejecting the invitation for one reason or another. The king then sends his armies to destroy the people who rejected his invitation, and he calls them murderers. Afterward, the king sends his servants into the highways to invite as many as they might find to the wedding, but one arrives without a wedding garment and is cast into outer darkness. To the casual reader, this sounds a little harsh, but it again demonstrates the need for God to divorce or put away anyone who would refuse or try to circumvent his plan of redemption. It was, after all, their choice to reject the Lord's salvation. We all need a garment for the wedding. We need to "put on Christ." The apostle Paul wrote: "For ye are all the children of God by faith in Christ Jesus. For as many of you as have been baptized into Christ have put on Christ" (Galatians 3:26–27). There must be both a "putting away" and a "putting on." But don't all religions have some validity? No! Apart from Christ, there is absolutely no hope and no redemption. People will not be allowed at the marriage of the Lamb without the applied righteousness of Christ on their lives. Jesus is "The Lord our Righteousness." Concerning a "righteous branch" that will be raised unto Israel's King, David, the Prophet Jeremiah wrote: "In his days Judah shall be saved, and Israel shall dwell safely: and this is his name whereby he shall be called, The Lord our righteousness" (Jeremiah 23:6). Salvation was offered to Israel, but it was not and is not forced on them.

Concerning Israel's need for salvation, the Apostle Paul wrote:

> Brethren, my heart's desire and prayer to God for Israel is, that they might be saved. For I bear them record that they have a zeal of God, but not according to knowledge. For they being ignorant of God's righteousness, and going about to establish their own righteousness, have not submitted themselves unto the righteousness of God.
>
> Romans 10:1–3

The parable of the ten virgins is a warning to be prepared because we don't know when the bridegroom is coming. The wise virgins had oil for their lamps and the foolish did not when the bridegroom arrived. The five wise virgins went with the bridegroom when he arrived, but as a result of their foolishness, the other five were excluded from the wedding celebration. In fact, the bridegroom told them, "I know you not" (Matthew 25:12b). Jesus was clearly teaching that there is a definite time limit on God's offer if one desires to participate in the celebration. Even though there were ten virgins to the one bridegroom, this has nothing to do with the practice of polygamy. It is a picture of Christ returning for his one and only bride that will consist of peoples of all nations, kindreds, and tongues. He's not going to wait forever for the world to come to its senses. In Psalm 14:1 and 53:1, David says: "The fool hath said in his heart, there is no God." This is the attitude that destroys all hope, and the foolish virgins thought they had plenty of time to get their oil when they were ready. The oil represents the Holy Spirit, and Scripture clearly states that if we are in the flesh we can't please God. The Scripture also says: "The Spirit itself beareth witness with our spirit, that we are the children of God: And if children, then heirs; heirs of God, and joint-heirs with Christ; if so be that we suffer with him, that we may be also glorified together" (Romans 8:16–17). A foolish and nonchalant attitude toward God will be more costly than anyone can imagine. God is going to put away this world and create a new one where righteousness will dwell. The Apostle Peter wrote: "But the day of the Lord will come as a thief in the night; in which the heavens shall pass away with a great noise, and the elements shall melt with fervent heat, the earth also and the works that are therein shall be burned up" (II Peter 3:10). Peter then wrote: "Nevertheless we, according to his promise, look for new heavens and new earth, wherein dwelleth righteousness" (II Peter 3:13)

Judgment is coming, and it will be more painful than the worst divorce the world has ever known. It will be final, forever. But it is not God's desire for any to perish in this fashion. Peter also said: "The Lord is not slack concerning his promise, as some men count slackness; but is longsuffering to us-ward, not willing that any should perish, but that all should come to the knowledge of repentance" (II Peter 3:9). Israel ignored all the signs and rejected all the warnings of God's prophets, and people continue to do the same today. People ignore and neglect their marriages, and they end in divorce, but no one seems to learn anything about God's will and God's plan that is seen in every failed marriage and in every good marriage.

Judgment will be the final great divorce! Everything bad and corrupted will be put away once and for all. God is in control! God has stated his case with a metaphor and with direct statements of what is required, and there are no excuses. Jesus said that nobody will come to the Father except by or though him. He is the way, the truth, and the life. There are those who would tell us that there are many paths to God, but God will tell us that there is only one, and that way is his Son, Jesus Christ. One of the simplest verses in the Bible is found in I John 5:12. I say that it is simple because every word used in the verse is a single syllable word, and it says: "He that hath the Son hath life; and he that hath not the Son of God hath not life." If people are trusting in their own goodness, their church, their religion, or anything other than the Son of God, they are trusting in the wrong thing. All the modern spirituality in the world will not get a single person into the Wedding Supper of the Lamb, and even if one were to find himself there, if he has not put on Christ, he will be cast into outer darkness.

THE NEW BRIDE

The church is the bride of Christ! God has already begun to call out his new bride after divorcing or "putting away" Israel. This new bride will be made up of people from every nation, including Israel. The Apostle John wrote:

> And they sung a new song, saying, Thou art worthy to take the book, and to open the seals thereof: for thou wast slain, and hast redeemed us to God by thy blood out of every kindred, and tongue, and people, and nation: and hast made us unto our God kings and priests: and we shall reign on the earth.
>
> Revelation 5:9–10

John the Baptist was the first in the New Testament to speak of the bride. The Baptist told his disciples: "He that hath the bride is the bridegroom: but the friend of the bridegroom, which standeth and heareth him, rejoiceth greatly because of the bridegroom's voice: this my joy is therefore fulfilled. He must increase and I

must decrease" (John 3:29–30). John had already identified Jesus as "the Lamb of God which taketh away the
sin of the world" in John 1:29, and now he was revealing
more about the Savior. Christ is the bridegroom, and
he is looking forward to a celebration, and John the
Baptist was already rejoicing with him. John seemed to
believe that the wedding was going to take place very
soon!

The customs of marriage at the time when Christ
was physically on the earth had three major parts. The
first step was the paying of the dowry to the parents of
the bride, creating an espousal that required a divorce
to terminate. A year later the bridegroom would come
for his bride, usually at night with a torch parade coming down the street, and at that time the bride would
return to the home of the bridegroom. Then the bride
and bridegroom would have a wedding feast or supper that might go on for days. Discussing Revelation
19:7–10, Walvoord writes: "In view of this custom, it
is significant that what is here announced is the wedding feast, or supper, and the implication is that the
first two steps of the wedding have taken place."[61]
Walvoord later says something that seems a little out
of character for his literal approach to Scripture. He
writes: "It should be remembered that this will not be a
literal feast with millions of people attending, but it is
a symbolic concept where the guests, or friends, of the
bride and bridegroom will join in on the celebration
of the marriage of the bridegroom and the bride."[62]
Walvoord believes that the wedding supper will take
place on the earth at the beginning of the millennial
reign when Jesus comes with all his saints. After the

mention of the marriage supper of the Lamb in which Walvoord sees a symbolic concept, he returns to his literal method of interpretation. Speaking of the New Jerusalem descending from heaven as a bride adorned for her husband, John Walvoord says:

> The city as described by John is a very impressive one even by present standards. Though some have said that the city is not a literal city and merely symbolizes the church, the Body of Christ, it seems best to consider it a literal city which, nevertheless, in its elements represents the church in some of its qualities.[63]
>
> Walvoord, 637

Since God cannot lie, whatever he says will happen, will certainly happen. It makes no difference what people believe or think they perceive. If God said it, that settles it. God will bring everything to fulfillment in the marriage supper of the Lamb, and the celebration will be fantastic, and when it all comes to pass, it will make perfect sense. Benjamin Keach wrote: "No bride ever appeared in such splendor, or so richly clothed and adorned, as the bride, the Lamb's wife shall, when the Marriage of the Lamb is come."[64] We may not be sure of where the supper will be or when it will take place, but you can be sure that it will occur, and it will be glorious.

At that time we will know and finally understand all the work that God has done to prepare us for our covenant or marriage relationship that will truly last forever. After all the different views that I have read in researching this book, it seems only appropriate to tell one more story that illustrates an ignorance of God's truth. This is not scripturally accurate, and I know it, but bear with me. A couple was on their way to the church to be married, and they were completely in love, but they died in a tragic accident along the way. When they arrived in heaven, they asked if they could be married since they missed their wedding on earth. The angel at the gate said he would check, and he was gone for what seemed an eternity. When he finally got back, he said that he had checked and gotten it approved, but the couple had a few reservations considering eternity, and they asked, "If it doesn't work out, may we get a divorce?" The angel responded, "No way! It took a really long time to find a preacher, and I don't know if I could ever find a lawyer."

The only marriage in heaven will be the marriage of the Lamb! Life is going to be so different! The Apostle John was searching for words to describe what he saw, and yet he was trying to express the unknowable in earthly terms as he was led by the Holy Spirit. Because of the varied interpretations of Revelation, I had a teacher at Howard Payne University who at one time said that he had only one sermon on the book. Its points were Jesus died; he rose again; he ascended into heaven; he is coming again; and we had better be ready.

Considering the customs of Israel concerning marriage, Walvoord says that the dowry has been paid at the cross, and the rapture of the church represents the bridegroom coming to receive his Bride, and the marriage supper will be the final stage of the marriage celebration. [65] One glaringly obvious difference between the arranged marriages of Israel and the marriage of the Lamb is that the Lamb's wife has to come to him of her own free will because she desires a special relationship with him. There are no arranged marriages for the Son of God, but, in another sense, there are. Teaching in the synagogue in Capernaum, Jesus said: "No man can come unto me, except the Father which hath sent me draw him: and I will raise him up at the last day" (John 6:44). We have free will, but we are only free to come to Christ when the spirit of God calls us to him. Perhaps this is partially why he ended the parable of the wedding feast with the statement: "Many are called, but few are chosen" (Matthew 22:14). Jesus began this story, which is a simile, by saying: "The kingdom of heaven is like unto a certain king, which made a marriage for his son, And sent forth his servants to call them that were bidden to the wedding: and they would not come" (Matthew 22:2–3). Jesus brought his message to the children of Israel, and for the most part, they rejected it. God had sent his prophets to declare his message, and they were persecuted and rejected as well. We have to remember, however, that almost all the early converts to Christianity after the coming of the Holy Ghost were Jews. It was not until the ministry of Paul as the apostle to the Gentiles that large numbers of Gentiles became believers and were added to the church. Tiring of the envious attitude of the Jews, we see the reaction of Paul and Barnabas in Acts 13:46. "Then Paul and Barnabas waxed bold, and said, It was necessary that the Word of God should first have been spoken to you: but seeing you put it from you, and judge yourselves unworthy of everlasting life, lo, we turn to the Gentiles." Look closely at this passage of scripture. Paul said that Israel "put it from" themselves. This sounds a lot like putting away as a man might "put away" his wife. Israel was, again, ignoring God and neglecting the call for an idea that seemed better to them. They had an idea of what Messiah was supposed to be, and Jesus did not fit their understanding of that idea. What kinds of ideas do you have about God, and where did those ideas originate? Is your belief system based on the Word of God or the words of men and women? We're talking about eternity here. Don't take any chances!

It is interesting that Paul, in his Epistle to the Romans, used the phrase: "to the Jew first," three times. It may be found in Romans 1:16, 2:9, and 2:10. Jesus' great commission was to go into the world and teach all *ethnicos*. This Greek word used in the great commission in Matthew 28:19 could literally be applied to mean all ethnic groups and the King James Version translates it as *nations*. Then, in Acts 1:8, just before the ascension, Jesus told his disciples to be his witnesses in Jerusalem, Judea, Samaria, and to the uttermost part of the earth. So, it had to begin with the Jews, but it was not God's plan to end there, and as we have seen from Revelation 5:9, the bride of Christ will be composed of every kindred, tongue, people, and nation. Becoming a Christian is metaphorically the same as accepting a proposal from God the Father in the person of the Holy Spirit on behalf of his Son. The group, *Good News Circle,* used to sing a song that had this line in it: "Anybody here want to live forever, Say I do." Well, do you want to live forever? Do you want to walk on golden streets? Are you sick and tired of living like you do, but you don't know what to do about it? There was a lot of insight in this old song, and it asked some good questions. God is calling out a people to a special relationship that begins here and now, but he won't continue asking forever. A decision has to be made! Make no mistake. Not deciding is a decision. Soren Kierkegaard wrote:

> Each person must choose between God and the world, God and mammon. This is the eternal unchangeable condition of choice that can never be evaded—no, never in all eternity. No one can say, "God and the world, they are not, after all, so absolutely different. One can combine them both in one choice." This is to refrain from choosing.[66]
>
> Kierkegaard, 10

We may choose God or the world, but we can't have both. To try to hold on to both would be spiritual adultery. The old song is telling us to say *I do* just as if we were in a wedding and pledging our love to God.

Picture the most glorious bride that you can possibly imagine, and understand that the bride that God is preparing will outshine her so much that she will appear as a filthy hag or a pile of dirt in comparison. God is preparing something that the Scripture says is beyond our understanding or imagination. He is preparing something that we have never seen or heard before. It will be totally different from this temporary, sin sick world. Paul wrote: "But it is written, Eye hath not seen, nor ear heard, neither have entered into the heart of man, the things which God hath prepared for them that love him" (I Corinthians 2:9).

The church is supposed to be the bride of Christ, but right now, let's face it, to the world, she isn't very pretty. There is only one church, and it is divided and scattered around the world because of geography and also because of theological differences. In many local churches, her love seems biased and cold, but when Christ returns, she is going to be changed forever and united into one glorious church that represents the bride of Christ. What a miracle! We should be working toward the goal of being like Christ right now. We don't know how much time is left, but right now is the time to consider the revelation of God's plan as it is pictured in this metaphor of marriage as he compares us to a chaste virgin prepared for his Son. Does your church appear to be like a virtuous woman, or does it more closely resemble Jezebel? Are we missing the point that God is trying to make? Our churches, marriages, and our families should reflect the glory of God. We should be walking testimonies of love to the world.

The scattering of God's people works to spread the gospel all over the world. An example of this may be seen early in the life of the church. Right after the stoning of Stephen, we may see that the church was scattered because of persecution but still spreading the gospel wherever they went.

> And Saul was consenting unto his death. And at that time there was a great persecution against the church which was at Jerusalem; and they were all scattered abroad throughout the regions of Judaea

and Samaria, except the apostles. And devout men carried Stephen to his burial, and made great lamentation over him. As for Saul, he made havock of the church, entering into every house, and haling men and women committed them to prison. Therefore they that were scattered abroad went every where preaching the word.

Acts 8:1–4

So, the church being scattered was not such a bad thing because God used it to spread the gospel outside of Jerusalem. Jesus had told his followers to be his witnesses in Jerusalem, Judaea, Samaria, and to the uttermost parts of the earth, and because of the devil's persecution the message was being spread. The devil meant it for evil, but God turned the tables on him and used it for good. Scattering of the church, then, is not really a bad thing, but the lack of unity within the church has been terribly damaging. We should be very careful about speaking evil of another local church, remembering that this group too is a part of the bride of Christ. They may not believe exactly as we do, but if they claim Christ as Lord and Savior, they are our brothers and sisters.

Many different groups of believers make a practice of regularly repeating what is referred to as the Lord's Prayer. I submit to you that what is being repeated is not the Lord's Prayer at all but a model prayer. Jesus had been asked to teach his followers how to pray. We may see this prayer in the following verses:

And it came to pass, that, as he was praying in a certain place, when he ceased, one of his disciples said unto him, Lord, teach us to pray, as John also taught his disciples. And he said unto them, When ye pray, say, Our Father which art in heaven, Hallowed be thy name. Thy kingdom come. Thy will be done, as in heaven, so in earth. Give us day by day our daily bread. And forgive us our sins; for we also forgive every one that is indebted to us. And lead us not into temptation; but deliver us from evil.

Luke 11:1–4

This was not a prayer that Jesus prayed. It was an example of how to pray. If you would like to see a prayer that belongs to the Lord, read chapter 17 of the gospel of John. This is what he prayed just before he was arrested and taken to be crucified. In the prayer of Jesus, he asks the Father to keep his followers unified. He said:

As thou hast sent me into the world, even so have I also sent them into the world. And for their sakes I sanctify myself, that they also might be sanctified through the truth. Neither pray I for these alone, but for them also which shall believe on me through their word; That they all may be one; as thou, Father, art in me, and I in thee, that they also may be one in us: that the world may believe that thou hast sent me. And the glory which thou gavest me I have given them; that they may be one, even as we are one: I in them, and thou in me, that they may be made perfect in one; and that the world may know that thou hast sent me, and hast loved them, as thou hast loved me. Father, I will that they also, whom thou hast given me, be with me where I am; that they may behold my glory, which thou hast given me: for thou lovedst me before the foundation of the world. O righteous Father, the world hath not known thee: but I have known thee, and these have known that thou hast sent me. And I have declared unto them thy name, and will declare it: that the love wherewith thou hast loved me may be in them, and I in them.

John 17:18–26

Here we see Jesus praying for the unity of those that the Father has given him and even for those he knows the Father will give him in the future. He prays for their sanctification and for their opportunity to see his glory and to experience his glory. He wants them to know his love. This is another portrait of the relationship that God desires to have with his people. As a husband and wife are supposed to be one, so Jesus desires for his people to be one. He wanted the church to be one with him as he is one with the Father, and he wants the church to be united as one to glorify the Father just as he plans to glorify the Father in his sacrificial death. He even reveals why he desires this by saying, "that the world may know that thou hast sent me." Our motivation should always center on God's love, which Christ, as the bridegroom, demonstrated for his chosen bride.

I have noticed something over the years that may be part of the problem. It is the use of fear and anger to motivate people to stand for a cause. I have received phone calls from people that I am sure are dedicated and think that they are doing God's work in protecting society and preserving the church, but they all use the same approach. They tell you that there is some vile thing on the horizon that is going to destroy family values or compromise the church, and then they ask for money. They may say something like, "We've got to fight the homosexual agenda, or the humanist agenda, or some other agenda before they ruin everything for us." Political action groups do the same thing, and the NRA, of which I have been a member, has perfected it. The church does not need to be motivated by fear. It needs to be motivated by love and compassion. God's plan is to preserve and protect a people for himself to be like a bride to his Son, and nothing and nobody can prevent it from coming to pass. Don't let fear and anger rule your life. As the bride, we are supposed to have only one Lord, and his name is Jesus. Be careful with whom you enter into an alliance, no matter how good their arguments and warnings sound. You might be making the same mistake that Israel made, and God called it adultery.

God offers us everlasting life and eternal joy, but many do not believe in eternity or the supernatural power of God. Many do not believe in God. What do they have to look forward to, and what hope do they have? Even among people who claim Christianity, some have thought death is the end, but, Christ conquered death and hell. Why would anyone think this life is all there is? Paul said: "If in this life only we have hope in Christ, we are of all men most miserable" (1 Corinthians 15:19). Kierkegaard wrote:

> If there were no eternal consciousness in man, if at
> the foundation of all there lay only a wildly seeth-
> ing power which writhing with obscure passions
> produced everything that is great and everything
> that is insignificant, if a bottomless void never
> satiated lay hidden beneath all—what then would
> life be but despair? [67]
>
> Kierkegaard, 10

If a person thinks that death is the end, then the
grave is this bottomless void. If there is no coming
judgment, then we may as well live like animals with
no ethics and no charity, but there is a God, and there
is hope of life everlasting as the bride of Jesus Christ.
God has provided victory for the believer, even in the
midst of defeat. Paul wrote to the church at Rome:

> Who shall separate us from the love of Christ?
> Shall tribulation, or distress, or persecution, or
> famine, or nakedness, or peril, or sword? As it is
> written, For thy sake we are killed all the day long;
> we are counted as sheep for the slaughter. Nay,
> in all these things we are more than conquerors
> through him that loved us...
>
> Romans 8:35–37

If martyrdom is our lot, we should be miserable if
in this life only we have hope in Christ, but Christ has
promised us a home with him forever. He has promised
to be with us always. We are his bride, and he loves us
and will take us to the home he has prepared for us.
Jesus said:

Let not your heart be troubled: ye believe in God, believe also in me. In my Father's house are many mansions: if it were not so, I would have told you. I go to prepare a place for you. And if I go and prepare a place for you, I will come again, and receive you unto myself; that where I am, there ye may be also.

John 14:1–3

You can consider this the vow of the bridegroom to the bride. He's coming back to receive those that are his. Will we be ready, waiting, and watching? What should the bride expect in the coming years? Paul wrote:

Let no man deceive you by any means: for that day shall not come, except there come a falling away first, and that man of sin be revealed, the son of perdition; who opposeth and exhalteth himself above all that is called God, or that is worshipped; so that he as God sitteth in the temple of God, shewing that he is God.

II Thessalonians 2:3–4

Paul had already written to the church at Thessalonica: "But ye, brethren, are not in darkness, that that day should overtake you as a thief" (I Thessalonians 5:4). The bride should not be surprised by the coming of the bridegroom, but she should rejoice as she sees the day approaching. Until he comes, we should be ministering to the least of these.

CONCLUSIONS AND PRACTICAL APPLICATION

What is God trying to communicate to his people with this obvious metaphor of marriage and divorce. John Gray writes in his book: "Falling in love is always magical. It feels eternal, as if love will last forever."[68] I don't think most people really fall in love as much as they fall in lust! Gary Thomas asks: "What if God designed marriage to make us holy more than to make us happy?"[69] Thomas then says: "I think most of us who have been married for any substantial length of time realize that the romantic roller coaster of courtship eventually evens out to the terrain of a Midwest interstate—long, flat stretches with an occasional overpass."[70] We are in a marathon. This is a long distance race, not a sprint. What is holding us back? Is it our ignorance or our apathy, or is it both? The Apostle Paul described our journey as a marathon, but most look at it as a short sprint. He wrote:

> Let us lay aside every weight, and the sin that doth
> so easily beset us, and let us run with patience the
> race that is before us, Looking unto Jesus the
> author and finisher of our faith; who for the joy
> that was set before him endured the cross, despis-
> ing the shame, and is set down at the right hand
> of the throne of God.
>
> Hebrews 12:1b-2

The things that hold us back need to be set aside for the race, and we should look to the example that Jesus has provided. The idea of a trophy wife or a trophy husband is ridiculous. Trophies are placed on shelves to collect dust and are seldom even looked at, and there is no companionship to be found with an inanimate object. There is only idolatry! The trophy we should strive for is the one we will be awarded in heaven in the very presence of God.

God's plan is to redeem us from the fall. The only way that this is possible is for us to humble ourselves as we admit our fallen state and by faith become one with him, and he uses the metaphor of marriage to help us understand, as much as is humanly possible, what kind of relationship he desires to have with us. In order to have a relationship with the Holy God, we have to be made holy, but as sinners, we all fall short of his requirement of absolute sinless perfection. The good news is that God has made a way that we may become presentable to himself through the work of the One who knew no sin and actually became sin for us. He uses the metaphor of divorce to illustrate what we will lose if we ignore his warnings. God wants his people to learn the truth about who they are, where they came from, and where they are going, but he also desires to help us along the way. He has placed signs all around us. He has invited us to experience his joy and his pain, and he wants to experience our joy and support us in our pain. He has tried to communicate with us on many levels and has painted word pictures so that we might better understand. In a world obsessed with the thrill of the moment and inundated with the concept of romanticism, a long relationship with God or anyone else sounds boring and tiresome to many people. People bounce from marriage to marriage or from relationship to relationship in search of happiness to no avail. The temporary happiness found in something new and different seems to be the only type of pleasure that the world can understand. There seems to be a pervasive playboy mentality throughout society. Gary Thomas said: "Romantic love has no elasticity to it. It can never be stretched; it simply shatters."[71] God wants us to learn about an eternal relationship, and we have difficulty with short-term relationships.

God gave us marriage as a metaphor to illustrate the life-long commitment that he desires to have with us in a covenant relationship, but this seems to be the furthest thing from most people's minds. Some people change partners like they trade cars, and when the new car smell dissipates or the new wears off, it's time to find a new one.

The Lord is still saying, "Whosoever will, may come." God presents an opened discussion that he plans to close in his own time and in his own way. Carl Vaught writes: "Metaphorical unity is an opened rela-

tion between two terms that is capable of endless artic-
ulation; and analogical separation is a relation between
two terms that binds them together and holds them
apart."[72] God has definitely articulated his position and
his plan since the beginning of time, but very few seem
to be listening. We will either be bound together with
him, or we will be held apart from him based upon
our response to the messages he sends. God wants us
to learn from the marriage metaphor and to become a
true and faithful "Bride" of Christ through the miraculous intervention of his Spirit as he leads us to fully
apply the Word to our hearts and in our lives. God is
speaking in so many different ways, but will the world
ever listen?

Just as many approach God's Word with an agenda
that they want to support or find proof texts for, many
also have their minds made up before coming to God
for answers due to some preconceptions that they find
very difficult to turn loose. Vaught also says: "That we
bring our own presuppositions to our philosophical task
ought to be admitted, but that those presuppositions
make responsible inquiry impossible is a philosophical thesis that must be rejected."[73] Why would anyone
involved in philosophy predetermine to reject an obviously sensible idea like this? Isn't philosophy supposed
to be about the search for truth and understanding?
Everyone has presuppositions and preconceived ideas.
To say that they do not influence a person is to lie to
one's self, but to admit that this makes responsible
inquiry impossible would reveal that in the flesh we
cannot be truly objective in exploring or discovering
anything without being influenced by those presuppo-

sitions. It is a matter of intellectual pride, and it will lead to death and separation from God. God is trying to communicate with us, and what he wants to deliver is absolute truth, but many philosophers disagree over the existence of absolute truth. When one speaks of philosophical progress or scientific progress, he or she is expressing a progress within the bounds and limitations of human understanding and observation. In many ways, humans are like ants trying to describe our universe, and we are limited by our own capacity to know and understand anything, much less everything. But what if the Creator of everything, with complete knowledge and wisdom, entered our tiny ant colony and revealed as much as we were able to comprehend and offered the presence of his Spirit to abide within each individual ant, thereby giving them greater understanding? How much would our presuppositions be worth in this instance? Paul warned the early church: "Beware lest any man spoil you through philosophy and vain deceit, after the tradition of men, after the rudiments of the world, and not after Christ" (Colossians 2:8). To the church at Rome, Paul also wrote:

> For the invisible things of him from the creation of the world are clearly seen, being understood by the things that are made, even his eternal power and Godhead; so that they are without excuse: Because that, when they knew God, they glorified him not as God, neither were thankful; but became vain in their own imaginations, and their foolish heart was darkened. Professing themselves to be wise, they became fools, and changed the image of the uncorruptible God into an image

like unto corruptible man, and to birds, and four-
footed beasts, and creeping things.

Romans 1:20–23

My conclusion is that we need to humble ourselves,
admitting that we actually know nothing, and we must
allow the Creator to reveal his truth to us about our
existence, our welfare, and our eternity. He has used
a metaphor involving something that is commonly
known (marriage), although not completely understood, to open our minds and hearts to a desired relationship that he offers for our welfare, preservation,
and eternity. He has pictured the alternative through
another metaphor (divorce), to warn us of the consequences of rejecting ultimate truth and deliverance
from our fallen state. He has made it abundantly clear
that judgment will take place, and we are responsible
for our actions and our inactions.

If, as the title to Gary Thomas' book, *Sacred
Marriage,* implies that marriage is supposed to be
sacred, what makes it sacred or holy? If it is just about
legalized procreation, why is it holy? If it is simply to
prevent sexual immorality and keep us from relapsing
back into bestiality as John Chrysostom said, how can
it be holy? First, God instituted marriage. It was not
man's creation, and it wasn't any human's idea for the
good of the social order. The church did not invent it,
and neither did any government. It is from God, and
that's what makes it sacred. Any time that God gives
us a gift, it is because he loves us and he desires to
bless us. Marriage, if it is not accepted as a gift of God,
can become a curse. If we misuse or distort the godly,

there will always be hell to pay. Secondly, when God gives us a gift, he wants us to accept it and use it for our own benefit and the benefit of others while growing the kingdom of God. There is much more to marriage than meets the eye of the casual observer, and sadly, many who enter marriage relationships seem to be casual observers. That is why divorce is so prevalent. So, how did God intend us to benefit from marriage? He wanted us to have an understanding of the relationship that he desires to have with us while demonstrating that relationship to the world through the married couple's relationship. And, when all is in submission to God's will according to God's plan, marriage is a priceless treasure to the whole family and to the community. I believe this could be why the devil is working overtime to destroy Christian marriages. He seems to understand it. Why don't we?

We hear a minister speak of the sanctity of marriage, and it is sometimes doubtful that even the minister understands what is being said. Do we preserve the sanctity of marriage by merely remaining loyal to our mate? Is not committing adultery the only thing necessary to preserve that sanctity? I believe that there is a great deal more to the sanctity than most people think. For marriage between a man and a woman to truly be sacred requires a total commitment, not only in fidelity to one's spouse, but also to God. God does not sanctify or make holy the unrepentant and profane. Marriage is a union between a man and a woman in the eyes of God for the purpose of edifying the church and growing his believers, while providing stability and security within the home and in society. How can a same-sex union ever hope to do this? They may hope to, but it will never happen. When accepting a gift from God, one must always accept it on God's terms and apply God's standards. I'm not campaigning against same-sex unions, but I don't like the idea of anyone calling it marriage because it subverts the message God is trying to deliver. Let me clearly state that I do not hate homosexuals. I know several of them. I love them all, but I am concerned about the lifestyle that prevents them from having a good relationship with God.

God gave us marriage for a very important reason, as we have already seen, and a same-sex marriage is an abomination in the eyes of God and makes a mockery of what God ordained marriage to be. Leviticus 18:22 says: "Thou shalt not lie with mankind, as with womankind: it is abomination." God says much the same thing about taking back a wife that has remarried in Deuteronomy 24:4. Proverbs 21:27 says: "The sacrifice of the wicked is abomination: how much more, when he bringeth it with a wicked mind." Jesus said: "Ye are they which justify yourselves before men; but God knoweth your hearts: for that which is highly esteemed among men is abomination in the sight of God" (Luke 16:15). God created male and female for a specific purpose, and it wasn't simply for sex and procreation. The New Testament mentions the degenerate condition of mankind and speaks of the many sins from which Christ died to redeem us. The Apostle Paul wrote to the church at Rome:

Wherefore God also gave them up to uncleanness through the lusts of their own hearts, to dishon-

our their own bodies between themselves: Who
changed the truth of God into a lie, and worshipped and served the creature more than the
Creator, who is blessed forever. Amen. For this
cause God gave them up to vile affections: for
even their women did change the natural use into
that which is against nature: And likewise also
the men, leaving the natural use of the woman,
burned in their lust one toward another; men with
men working that which is unseemly, and receiving in themselves that recompense of their error
which was meet.

Romans 1:24–27

The really good news for the entire world may be
found in Paul's letter to the church at Corinth:

Know ye not that the unrighteous shall not
inherit the kingdom of God? Be not deceived:
neither fornicators, nor idolaters, nor adulterers,
nor effeminate, nor abusers of themselves with
mankind, Nor thieves, nor covetous, nor drunk-
ards, nor revilers, nor extortioners, shall inherit
the kingdom of God. And such were some of you:
but ye are washed, but ye are sanctified, but ye are
justified in the name of the Lord Jesus, and by the
Spirit of our God.

I Corinthians 6:9–11

Why is this good news? It is good news because
it doesn't matter what anyone has done or who they
have been sleeping with; God offers to wash them and
cleanse them soul-deep with the blood of Jesus Christ

and to sanctify and justify them making them a child of the King.

I have had some strange requests over the years concerning weddings. I have done them outside, in various buildings of the church, in homes, and I have even done one under water in a YMCA pool at the request of a couple that loved scuba diving and wanted to remember their special day. I tied the ceremony to baptism and explained that they were starting a new life, and in a sense, they had died to an old way of life and had come up out of the water to truly live in newness of life. I have concluded that a couple's "special day" is not so much about the location of the ceremony, the method, or even the words that are all too soon forgotten, but about the couple's relationship and commitment to God and to one another.

When, where, and how will God have the marriage supper of the Lamb? It really doesn't matter to me as long as I am there. Be assured that it will happen in God's timing, at God's chosen location, and according to God's will. But, on earth, people generally do as they please, and God is often an afterthought or someone to call on when we have messed things up beyond our capacity to "fix it." Until we are with him in glory, we should take advantage of every opportunity to rely on the One who knows and understands all the difficulties that we face, and who knows and sees all the pitfalls that lie ahead. Paul wrote: "This I say then, walk in the Spirit, and ye shall not fulfill the lust of the flesh" (Galatians 5:16).

Being led by the spirit of God is an awesome privilege, but for many, it is usually not a priority. Many believe that God created the world and then stepped aside to let nature take its course. But God has continually tried to communicate with us through this metaphor of marriage, and he literally stepped into his creation as one of us to pay the dowry for our betrothal so that we might be made pure, holy, and acceptable to him and so that we might be joined to him for all eternity. The world, the flesh, and the devil would love to cheapen marriage and cause us to miss the blessing that God has prepared for us.

Since marriage is a word picture or a metaphor of what God desires to have with us, we must be careful to communicate this to our children and our children's children. The church needs to understand the importance of marriage and its eternal significance. We need to take it more seriously and take time with prospective brides and grooms, explaining the significance of the commitment that they are about to make, and we need to nurture their relationships within the church family. Even the government of the United States is beginning to see the importance of premarital counseling; however, from whom will this counsel come? The book of Psalms begins: "Blessed is the man that walketh not in the counsel of the ungodly, nor standeth in the way of sinners, nor sitteth in the seat of the scornful. But his delight is in the Lord; and in his law doth he meditate day and night" (Psalm 1:1–2). God's counsel is always true and holy, and he has been trying to give his expert advice to the church for years. Time is running out for a world that is lost and dying, and in order for the church to reach this world, we need to understand the relationship that Christ offers, and we need to live out our lives, communicating truth in love to those who are blinded by their own rebellion against God and his will. It is my prayer that believers will take a long, close look at their own marriage relationships and consider how those marriages are glorifying God, or if they are detracting from God's message. Marriage is about making adjustments, but some need a complete overhaul. There is hope for any marriage if the couple will commit their relationship to God in love, each considering the other's needs, and in so doing, the church will have the joy of seeing a picture of a relationship that God desires to have with his people.

Returning now to the prophecy of Jesus concerning his Second Coming in the book of Matthew, let us recall the wording that he used to describe the times. He said of the times of Noah: "…they were eating and drinking, marrying and giving in marriage, until the day that Noe entered into the ark, and knew not until the flood came, and took them all away; so shall also the coming of the Son of man be" (Matthew 24:38b - 39). Does this simply mean that everyone will be surprised at Christ's return? I think that there is more to this than meets the eye, and when Jesus put marriage into this prophecy, he was again pointing to an overlooked revelation of God. When we consider the metaphoric meaning of marriage, Christ is saying that there is an obvious revelation right in front of everyone's eyes that points directly to God, and they are taking it for granted and missing the message. We could equate this with someone attending church services all their lives, sitting through hundreds of invitations to receive Christ without doing so, and then believing that they are okay because they regularly attend church. The fact that all the commentaries I examined on this particular verse pretty much agreed that this is a warning of the suddenness and surprise of the coming judgment also convinces me that this has been overlooked for years, and it is still being overlooked. With all the mention of marriage and divorce and the thread that so many agree appears in the Bible concerning the metaphor of marriage relating to both Israel and the church, one would think that when marriage is mentioned by Christ, we would take a close look at what is being said. But we haven't. Eating and drinking are necessary for the physical body to survive, but who provides this food and drink? This is also a revelation, and we should remember that God sends the rain and prevents famine and drought. A person can survive without being married. Eating and drinking are normal daily routines, but what about marriage and giving in marriage? We don't get married every day, and we don't offer or give our daughters in marriage every day. Hopefully, and by God's grace, these are once in a lifetime occurrences. So, why did Jesus include eating and drinking with marrying and giving in marriage? Just as food and drink are gifts from God, so is marriage. It is a gift that points to the relationship that God wants to have with every person. Remember that he is longsuffering and not willing that any should perish but that all should come to repentance.

When you consider the use by God of the marriage metaphor in revealing his plan for Israel and the church, there is obvious irony to be found in this statement. The people will be doing something on a regular basis that should be pointing them to the redemptive work of Christ, and they won't even realize it! The world will be almost completely fallen away from the truth that was proclaimed by the Savior and his church when he returns. Paul describes the world in Romans 1:28–32, and he gives his description in past tense. This is one long sentence, and we will not quote it all here, but I challenge you to read the whole first chapter of Romans and consider the implications for our world today. Verse 28 says: "And even as they did not like to retain God in their knowledge, God gave them over to a reprobate mind, to do those things which are not convenient." Why would anyone not want to retain God in their knowledge? Since there is a God, shouldn't we be responsible to him? But people do not want to be responsible. We have a natural fallen tendency to want to blame something or someone else for our shortcomings. Not much has changed since those days in Eden immediately after the fall.

If we don't always retain God in our knowledge, we will miss the signs and revelations that he has placed before us. Marriage is a huge sign! As Jesus mentions marriage in Matthew 24, he is again placing before our ears and eyes this word picture of a relationship that can only find perfection in God. But if teachers simply pass over this verse and say that it is merely suggesting that life will be going on as usual when Christ returns, how are the students supposed to grasp the meaning? After considering the metaphor of marriage and divorce that God uses as a gigantic sign to point to a desired relationship, from this point on we should very carefully consider the word "marriage" every time we see it in Scripture, and we should consider the full implications of its use. We should also think of coming judgment every time we see "putting away" or "divorce" mentioned in God's Word.

When Jesus describes the end times and says that they will be "marrying and giving in marriage," we should almost be able to hear the sound of sadness in his voice. God began in Genesis with a marriage, continued in the giving of the law, calling himself jealous, repeated it through the prophets with more imagery pointing out idolatry and describing it as harlotry, began the ministry of Jesus at a wedding, described the church's relationship with Christ as his bride, used it as a teaching tool for Jesus in parables, and will finalize all his plan of redemption with the marriage supper of the Lamb. What else does he need to do to convince us? He provides the food we eat and the water we drink, and many take it for granted that there will always be food and water. Most do not thank him for daily sustenance but consider nature and their own hard work or, in some cases, the hard work of others as their security. Many will never learn or accept the truth that God has revealed his plan for humanity, and it is not just a plan of hope; it is a plan that is full of assurance.

Jesus said: "Come unto me all ye who labour and are heavy laden, and I will give you rest" (Matthew 11:28). The prophet Isaiah, speaking for God, had said: "Incline your ear, and come unto me: hear, and your soul shall live; and I will make an everlasting covenant with you, even the sure mercies of David" (Isaiah 55:3). Then, Isaiah said:

> Seek ye the Lord while he may be found, call upon him when he is near: Let the wicked forsake his way, and the unrighteous man his thoughts: and let him return unto the Lord, and he will have mercy upon him; and to our God, for he will abundantly pardon. For my thoughts are not your thoughts, neither are your ways my ways, saith the Lord.
>
> Isaiah 55:6–8

God knew and still knows that there is a serious communication gap between the world and himself. He has communicated his desired relationship from the very beginning. Will we listen, or will we ignore his message? As believers in the Lord Jesus, we should have our minds renewed. The Apostle Paul wrote: "For who hath known the mind of the Lord, that he may instruct him? But we have the mind of Christ" (I Corinthians 2:16). Since believers have the mind of Christ, we should have renewed minds as Paul wrote in Ephesians 4:23–24, and we should "put on the new man" that is "created in righteousness and holiness."

The practical application of the knowledge that we acquire about marriage has been expressed in the last few paragraphs, and its meaning should be self-evident. Here is a brief recap of the application. Believers should guard their marriages and nurture them as an example to others of the relationship that God desires to have with all who will come to him freely. The meaning and significance of a Christian marriage should be clearly explained to all prospective brides and grooms before the wedding. We should teach our children the significance of marriage. When we face difficulties within a relationship, we should seek godly counsel. We should offer counsel to others in need in a spirit of meekness. Husbands and wives should listen to God and study his Word together, and they should regularly thank God for the gift of marriage. We should heed Paul's advice to "set aside every weight and the sin that so easily besets us." We should guard or hearts and minds and remain loyal to our mates.

Couples should work to improve their marriages so that others might readily see the picture of God's desired relationship. The marriage relationship should be kept holy, and couples should be very careful not to bring anything into it that might defile it. We should remember that marriage is a gift from God and treat it as such. Humility is a must, and you do not always have to be right. When one stumbles and sins, he or she should immediately confess that sin to God and repent or turn from it, striving to never do it again. We should know our limitations and remain within the boundaries that God has set for us. Marriage was designed for companionship, and it should glorify God. If God is not being glorified in your marriage, what are you willing to do to change?

The Apostle Paul wrote to the church at Rome concerning their deliverance from sin and their need to rely on God's grace rather than the Law of Moses:

> Know ye not, brethren, (for I speak to them that know the law,) how that the law hath dominion over a man as long as he liveth? For the woman which hath an husband is bound by the law to

her husband so long as he liveth; but if the husband is dead, she is loosed from the law of her husband. So then if, while her husband liveth, she be married to another man, she shall be called an adulteress: but if her husband is dead, she is free from the law; so that she is no adulteress, though she be married to another man. Wherefore, my brethren, ye also are become dead to the law by the body of Christ, that ye should be married to another, even to him who is raised from the dead, that we should bring forth fruit unto God. For when we were in the flesh, the motions of sins, which were by the law, did work in our members to bring forth fruit unto death. But now are we delivered from the law, that being dead wherein we were held; that we should serve in newness of spirit, and not in oldness of the letter.

Romans 7:1–6

Paul spoke of the laws of marriage to reveal a truth to the believers in Rome almost two thousand years ago that many still do not understand today. The law has dominion over a person as long as they live! In chapter six, Paul has already stated: "For sin shall not have dominion over you: for ye are not under the law, but under grace" (Romans 6:14). It is interesting that Paul begins chapter seven speaking to the "brethren," but he then speaks of the "woman" to explain the relationship that God desires to have with the "brethren." Israel had been the espoused wife of God in the Old Testament, and now the church is being prepared as the Bride of Christ. Is this, then, a discourse for New Testament times about marriage and how divorce causes a woman to become an adulteress? No! Paul is not writing a new law for the church. He is explaining that we cannot be justified by the law, and we should be dead to the law in order to legitimately be married to another. Remember that this was being explained to the brethren. Was Paul endorsing homosexuality? No! He was speaking of a relationship that both men and women may have with the Lord Jesus Christ that God has been working to reveal through his Word from the very beginning. He was describing a companionship that is perfect, pure, and holy that has been made possible through the shed blood of the Lord Jesus Christ.

Many Christians today are inordinately binding themselves to the law. Paul wrote: "Know ye not, that whom ye yield yourselves servants to obey, his servants ye are to whom ye obey; whether of sin unto death, or obedience unto righteousness?" (Romans 6:16). The law never saved anyone. It revealed our need for salvation and the method of that salvation through the blood. Jesus fulfilled the law. No more sacrifices are necessary to purchase our salvation, and keeping feasts and following the law will not get anyone into heaven. We need a relationship with God that has been revealed and made available through what Christ did on Calvary and through the power of his resurrection. God is seeking a bride for his Son that will be redeemed from every nation, kindred, and tongue. Don't get caught up in legalities. Allow yourself to be truly set free in Christ Jesus. You can be free from the law, free from sin, and free from death. The biggest question that you will ever face in this life is: "What will you do with Jesus?"

After dealing with the hardness of the Pharisees' hearts, Jesus was alone with his disciples, and they asked him about what he had told the Pharisees concerning divorce. Jesus told them: "Whosoever shall put away his wife, and marry another, committeth adultery against her. And if a woman shall put away her husband, and be married to another, she committeth adultery" (Mark 10:11–12). This is especially interesting since in Jesus' day, a woman did not have the option to put away her husband, but Jesus stated this as if she did. Many in the church have taken this teaching that Christ delivered to his disciples and applied it as a new law for the church in such a way that people are excluded from the fellowship of the church. Is that what Christ intended for us to do? I think that he was expressing to his followers the importance of the sanctity of marriage, and he understood what he was saying far more than they did. He was trying to prepare a bride for himself, and this would make more sense to them later when they received the Holy Spirit. No man or woman should ever consider putting away their opportunity for a relationship with Christ, but many not only consider it; they do it. We live in a world that does not like to retain God in its knowledge. Many are just too busy for him, but there is a payday some day. Ephesians says that the wages of sin is death. Rejecting God's gift is sin, and a person will earn wages from that sin. Payday is on the way. God is offering us a free gift that we cannot earn or ever hope to buy in place of these wages of sin. The gift he offers is eternal life in Jesus Christ.

We need to remember what Christ has saved us from and what he is directing us to be and do. Christianity has been reduced by many to sound like a get out of hell free card. It is really about a covenant relationship that costs a person all that they have and all that they are but rewards them with more than they can imagine. Don't misunderstand. I'm not saying that anyone can purchase their salvation. I'm saying that God has a purpose for each of his redeemed children that involves sacrifice and commitment to his kingdom. When we consider the number of martyrs and those who have been tortured for their faith, those who have gone hungry, and those who have suffered tremendous personal loss and yet kept their faith, we must conclude that this relationship with God in Christ Jesus is definitely for better or for worse in this life. This sacrifice and commitment is like a marriage covenant, and it truly is also for richer or for poorer in sickness and in health. What we used to consider as ours is now God's, but considering the price Christ paid to redeem us, we should willingly place everything at his feet. Remember what Jesus said to the rich young ruler.

> Now when Jesus heard these things, he said unto him, Yet lackest thou one thing: sell all that thou hast, and distribute unto the poor, and thou shalt have treasure in heaven: and come, follow me. And when he heard this, he was very sorrowful: for he was very rich.
>
> Matthew 18:22–23

We don't have a set of rules to obey to earn or maintain our salvation. We have the grace of God, and we should remember that he left heaven to be born of a virgin, giving up all authority to submit himself to earthly parents and was totally submissive to the will of his heavenly Father. He gave everything for us. What are we willing to sacrifice, and what burdens are we willing to bear? If we place our trust in the Lord Jesus Christ, we have a covenant relationship with God that involves the indwelling Holy Spirit to lead and guide us every step of the way. We have the written Word of God by which we may determine the right path and the Light of the World to lead the way. None of us can rightfully claim any righteousness of our own. All our righteousness comes from God through the shed blood of Jesus Christ. Any self-righteousness is an insult to God and a most horrendous sin. Without his presence we are nothing. Jesus said: "I am the vine, ye are the branches: He that abideth in me, and I in him, the same bringeth forth much fruit: for without me ye can do nothing" (John 15:5).

We need this covenant relationship. We need to understand the commitment, and we desperately need to understand how serious God is about coming to him on his terms. We can't see tomorrow, but he can. We don't know the pitfalls that are ahead of us, but he does. We don't have the strength or the ability to save ourselves, but he does. He loves us in spite of our sin and rebellion. Will you come to him forsaking all others? Are you willing to share your life, your love, your decisions, and all your possessions with him? The really good news about this marriage is that there is no "until death do us part." Death is just the beginning of eternity with him and the biggest celebration anyone has ever seen.

BIBLICAL THREAD
OF THE METAPHOR

Genesis 2:18-25	Bone of my bone and flesh of my flesh, cleave and be one flesh
Exodus 34:11-16	Make no covenants in the land lest sons and daughters go whoring
Leviticus 17:7	No more sacrifice to devils after whom they have gone whoring
Leviticus 20:4-6	No whoring after Molech, familiar spirits, and wizards
Numbers 5:11-31	Offering for spirit of jealousy
Numbers 15:38	Don't follow your heart and eyes to go a whoring
Deuteronomy 4:24	Jealous God and a consuming fire
Deuteronomy 5:9	Jealous God
Deuteronomy 6:15	Jealous God and angry
Deuteronomy 32:16	God provoked to jealousy
Deuteronomy 32:21	Moved God to jealousy with and provoked his anger
Joshua 24:15-20	Choose to obey God, he is Jealous and he will punish idolatry
Judges 2:16-17	Whoring after other gods
Judges 8:33	Whoring after Baalim and made Baalberith their god
Ruth 4:1-14	Kinsman redeemer, Boaz marries Ruth
I Kings 19:10-14	Elijah jealous for God because of Israel's abominations
I Chronicles 5:25	Whoring after the gods of the people of the land
II Chronicles 21:13	Whoring like the whoredoms of the house of Ahab
Psalm 78:58	Provoked God to anger and jealousy with idolatry
Psalm 106:39	Whoring with their own inventions
Proverbs 6:32	Commit adultery and destroy your own soul
Hosea 2:7-8	Israel uses blessings from God to court Baal and God will take it all away
Hosea 2:19	In the future God will betroth Israel to himself forever with people that weren't his
Hosea 4:11	Whoredom and wine take away thy heart
Hosea 4:14	The people that do not understand shall fall because of whoredoms and adultery
Isaiah 1:21	Faithful city become a harlot and full of murderers
Isaiah 57:3-9	Sons of sorceress, seed of adulterer and the whore, gone up to another
Isaiah 62:1-5	As the bridegroom rejoices over the bride, God will rejoice over you and the Land will be called Beulah (married)
Jeremiah 2:1-2	Remember the love of thine espousals and your holiness unto the Lord
Jeremiah 2:20	But you played the harlot
Jeremiah 2:23-24	You are a swift dromedary and a wild ass used to the wilderness
Jeremiah 2:32	You have forgotten me days without number
Jeremiah 3:1-2	You have played the harlot with many lovers, but return to me, polluted with whoredoms
Jeremiah 3:8-9	Backsliding Israel commits adultery and God divorces her

Jeremiah 5:7	Assembled themselves by troops in harlot's houses
Jeremiah 7:9	Commit adultery and burn incense to Baal
Jeremiah 23:14	False prophets are adulterous and likened to Sodom and Gomorrah
Ezekiel 16:31	A harlot who refuses pay
Ezekiel 16:32	As a wife that commits adultery
Ezekiel 23:37	Adultery and caused their sons to pass through the fire
Micah 1:7	Samaria will be punished and all idols destroyed, return to the hire of a harlot
Matthew 9:15	Jesus is the Bridegroom
Matthew 12:38-39, 16:4	Evil and adulterous generation seeks a sign
Matthew 22:1-14	Parable of the marriage of the king's son
Matthew 25:1-12	Parable of the virgins
Mark 2:19-20	Jesus is the Bridegroom
Mark 8:38	Adulterous and sinful generation
Mark 13:22	False christs and false prophets will try to seduce with signs and wonders
Luke 14:16-24	The parable of the great supper (Picture of the marriage supper of the Lamb)
John 2:1-11	Marriage at Cana, beginning of miracles
John 3:28-30	John the Baptist says Jesus is the Bridegroom and his joy is fulfilled
Romans 7:1-5	Married to another, dead to the law but alive in grace
I Corinthians 6:15-18	Church not to join with harlots, we are one spirit with the Lord
II Corinthians 11:1-3	Godly jealousy, espoused to one husband
Galatians 5:16	Walk in the Spirit so as not to fulfill the lust of the flesh
Ephesians 5:25	Love your wife as Christ loved the church and gave himself for it
Ephesians 5:30-33	We are flesh of Christ's flesh and bone of his bones
Hebrews 13:4	Marriage is honorable, but God will judge adulterous
James 4:4	The church's adultery - friendship with the world
I John 2:16-17	Lust of the flesh, lust of the eyes, the pride of life is of the world and will pass
I John 2:26	Warning against seduction
I John 2:28-29	Abide in him, we've been adopted into the family
I John 3:2-3	Abide in him or remain chaste and loyal
Revelation 19:2-3	The great whore judged, human society give totally to lust
Revelation 19:7-9	Marriage supper of the Lamb
Revelation 21:2	New Jerusalem adorned as a bride for her husband
Revelation 21:9	The Bride, the Lamb's wife
Revelation 22:17	The Spirit and the Bride say come

There are many more verses that could have been cited demonstrating God's attempt to reveal his desired relationship through the metaphor of marriage and metaphor of divorce or separation from God, but this is a good place to start a study and should be convincing enough that God is definitely attempting to communicate an important truth.

ENDNOTES

Metaphors of Life

1   Bernard Ramm, *Protestant Biblical Interpretation A Textbook of Hermeneutics,* Third Revised Edition, Baker Book House, Grand Rapids, Michigan, sixth printing 1974, p. 143.

2   Josh McDowell, *The New Evidence That Demands A Verdict,* Thomas Nelson Publishers, Nashville, Tennessee, 1999, p. 340.

3   Alfred Edersheim, *The Life and Times of Jesus the Messiah,* William B. Eerdmans Publishing Co., Grand Rapids, Michigan, 1971, p. 353.

4   Ibid., p. 353.

5   John Gray, Ph.D., *Men Are From Mars, Women Are From Venus,* Harper Collins Publishers, New York, New York, 1992, p. 10.

6   Ibid., p. 9.

7   Lewis Sperry Chafer, *Major Bible Themes 52 Vital Doctrines of the Scripture Simplified and Explained,* Revised by John F. Walvoord; Zondervan

Publishing House, Grand Rapids, Michigan, 1974, p.278.

8   John Gray, Ph. D., *Men Are From Mars, Women Are From Venus*, p. 10.

The Keys to Communication

9   Dietrich Bonhoeffer, *The Cost of Discipleship*, Revised and Unabridged Edition, Macmillan Publishing Company, New York, New York, Eighteenth printing, 1976, p. 99.

10   Ibid., p. 97.

11   Christl M. Maier, *Daughter Zion, Mother Zion*, Fortress Press, Minneapolis, Minnesota, 2008, p. 96.

12   C. S. Lewis, *The Great Divorce*, The Macmillan Company, New York, New York, Fifteenth Printing, 1966, p. 36.

13   Ibid., p. 36.

14   Ibid., p. 36.

15   U. S. *Constitution*, Amendment I.

16   William M. Pinson, Jr., *Baptists and Religious Liberty*, Baptist Way Press, Dallas, Texas, 2007, p. 70.

17   Gray, John, Ph.D., *Men Are From Mars, Women Are From Venus*, p. 56.

18   Thomas White, "Adoption The Heart of the Gospel," *Southwestern News*, Southwestern Baptist Theological Seminary Communications

Group, Forth Worth, Texas, Winter 2009, Volume 67, No. 2, p. 8.

19 Ibid., p.8.

Origin of Divorce and the Ongoing Problem

20 Lewis Sperry Chafer, *Major Bible Themes 52 Vital Doctrines of the Scripture Simplified and Explained,* Revised by John F. Walvoord; Zondervan Publishing House, Grand Rapids, Michigan, 1974, p. 278.

21 Soren Kierkegaard, Charles E. Moore, ed., Provocations, Spiritual Writings of Kierkegaard, Orbis Books, Maryknoll, New York, 2007, p. 119.

22 Gushee, David P., "Who Needs A Covenant," *Marriage, Christian Reflection A Series in Faith and Ethics,* General Editor Robert B. Kruschwitz, Published by The Center for Christian Ethics, Baylor University, One Bear Place, Waco Texas, 2006, p. 13.

23 Leland Ryken, James C. Wilhoit, Tremper Longman, III, editors, *Dictionary of Biblical Imagery,* InterVarsity Press, Downers Grove, Illinois, 1998, p. 213.

24 Jay E. Adams, *Marriage, Divorce, and Remarriage in the Bible,* p. 28.

25 Bill and Lindi McCartney, *Sold Out Becoming Man Enough To Make A Difference,* Word Publishing, Nashville, Tennessee, 1997, p. 210.

Celibacy, Other Than Sex, What Is Missing?

26   J. N. D. Kelly, *Golden Mouth: The Story of John Chrysostom Ascetic, Preacher, Bishop,* Baker Books, Grand Rapids, Michigan, 1995, p. 3.

27   Georgia Harkness, *John Calvin The Man and His Ethics,* Parthenon Press, Nashville, Tennessee, 1931, p. 133.

28   J. N. D. Kelly, *Golden Mouth: The Story of John Chrysostom Ascetic, Preacher, Bishop,* p. 23.

29   Ibid., p. 23.

30   Ibid., p. 23.

31   Ibid., p.64.

32   Thomas, Gary L., *Sacred Marriage,* Zondervan, Grand Rapids, Michigan, 2000, p.238.

33   Ibid., p. 50.

34   Ibid., p. 82.

35   Ibid., p. 82.

36   Ibid., p. 21.

37   Bill Bright; Edwin Cole; Dr. James Dobson; Tony Evans; Bill McCartney; Luis Palau; Randy Phillips; Gary Smalley; Jack Hayford; Boone Wellington; Glen E. Wagner; Howard Hendricks; Gary Oliver; Jerry Kirk; Dale Schlafer; H. B. London, Jr.; Phillip Porter; Gordon England, *Seven Promises of a Promise Keeper,* Focus on the Family Publishing, Colorado Springs, Colorado, 1994, p. 8.

Desired Relationship

38 Ryken, Leland; Wilhoit, James C.; Longman, Tremper, III; editors, *Dictionary of Biblical Imagery*, InterVarsity Press, Downers Grove, Illinois, 1998, p. 538.

39 Ibid., pp. 538–539.

40 Edersheim, Alfred, *The Life and Times of Jesus the Messiah*, pp. 352–353.

41 Ortlund, Raymond C., Jr., *God's Unfaithful Wife*, p. 30.

42 Ibid., p. 30.

43 Gary L. Thomas, *Sacred Marriage*, p. 35.

44 Ibid., p. 97.

45 Craig S. Keener, ... And *Marries Another, Divorce and Remarriage in the Teaching of the New Testament*, Hendrickson Publishers, Peabody, Massachusetts, 1991.

46 George M. Lamsa, *Idioms In the Bible Explained and A Key to the Original Gospels*, Harper and Row, Publishers, San Francisco, 1985.

47 Ibid., p. 98.

48 Ibid., p. 98.

49 Rubel Shelly, *Divorce & Remarriage A Redemptive Theology*, Leafwood Publishers, Abilene, Texas, 2007, p. 10.

50 Ibid., p. 10.

The Unfaithful Wife of God

51 John F. Walvoord, *Every Prophecy of the Bible*, Chariot Victor Publishing, Colorado Springs, Colorado, 1999, p. 122.

52 Ibid., p. 282.

53 Ortlund, Raymond C., Jr., *God's Unfaithful Wife*, p. 45.

54 Ibid., p. 91.

55 Ibid., p. 93.

56 Ibid., p. 93.

57 Ibid., p. 26.

58 O'Brien, Julia M., *Challenging Prophetic Metaphor: Theology and Ideology in the Prophets*, p. 30.

59 Ibid., p. 31.

60 Ibid., p. 35.

God's Divorce Case

There are no endnotes for this chapter.

The New Bride

61 John Walvoord, *Every Prophecy of the Bible*, p. 617.

62 Ibid., p. 618.

63 Ibid., p. 637.

64 Benjamin Keach, *Preaching From the Types and Metaphors of the Bible*, Kregel Publications, Grand Rapids, Michigan, 1972, p. 963.

65 John Walvoord, *Every Prophecy of the Bible*, pp. 617- 618.

66 Soren Kierkegaard, Charles E. Moore, ed., Provocations, Spiritual Writings of Kierkegaard, Orbis Books, Maryknoll, New York, 2007, p. 10.

67 Soren Kierkegaard, *Fear and Trembling*, A & D Publishing, Radford, Virginia, Wilder Publications, 2008, p. 10.

Conclusions and Practical Application

68 John Gray, Ph.D., *Men Are From Mars, Women Are From Venus A Practical Guide for Improving Communication and Getting What You Want in Your Relationship*, p. 13.

69 Gary L. Thomas, *Sacred Marriage*, Zondervan, Grand Rapids, Michigan, 2000, p. 13.

70 Ibid., p. 16.

71 Ibid., p. 15.

72 Carl G. Vaught, Metaphor, *Analogy, and the Place of Places Where Religion and Philosophy Meet*, Baylor University Press, Waco, Texas, 2004, p. 66.

73 Ibid., p. 18.

BIBLIOGRAPHY

Adams, Jay E., *Marriage, Divorce, and Remarriage in the Bible,* Zondervan, Grand Rapids, Michigan, 1980.

Bonhoeffer, Dietrich, *The Cost of Discipleship,* Revised and Unabridged Edition, Macmillan Publishing Company, New York, New York, Eighteenth printing, 1976.

Bright, Bill; Cole, Edwin; Dobson, Dr. James; Evans, Tony; McCartney, Bill; Palau, Luis; Phillips, Randy; Smalley, Gary; Hayford, Jack; Wellington, Boone; Wagner, Glen E.; Hendricks, Howard; Oliver, Gary; Kirk, Jerry; Schlafer, Dale; London, H. B., Jr.; Porter, Phillip; England, Gordon, *Seven Promises of a Promise Keeper,* Focus on the Family Publishing, Colorado Springs, Colorado, 1994.

Chafer, Lewis Sperry, *Major Bible Themes 52 Vital Doctrines of the Scripture Simplified and Explained,* Revised by John F. Walvoord; Zondervan Publishing House, Grand Rapids, Michigan, 1974.

Chapman, Gary, An excerpt from: *The Transformation of a Man's Heart,* "Role Extremes," *Men of Integrity Your Daily Guide to the Bible and Prayer,*

January/February, 2009, Pg. 42, Tuesday, February 10 - Daily Devotional, "Marriage is a Team Sport."

Edersheim, Alfred, *The Life and Times of Jesus the Messiah,* William B. Eerdmans Publishing Co., Grand Rapids, Michigan, 1971.

Gray, John, Ph.D., *Men Are From Mars, Women Are From Venus A Practical Guide for Improving Communication and Getting What You Want in Your Relationship,* Harper Collins Publishers, New York, New York, 1992.

Gushee, David P., "Who Needs A Covenant," *Marriage, Christian Reflection A Series in Faith and Ethics,* General Editor Robert B. Kruschwitz, Published by The Center for Christian Ethics, Baylor University, One Bear Place, Waco Texas, 2006.

Harkness, Georgia, *John Calvin The Man and His Ethics,* Parthenon Press, Nashville, Tennessee, 1931.

Keach, Benjamin, *Preaching From the Types and Metaphors of the Bible,* Kregel Publications, Grand Rapids, Michigan, 1972.

Kelly, J. N. D., *Golden Mouth: The Story of John Chrysostom Ascetic, Preacher, Bishop,* Baker Books, Grand Rapids, Michigan, 1995.

Keener, Craig S., *…And Marries Another Divorce and Remarriage in the Teaching of the New Testament,* Hendrickson Publishers, Peabody, Massachusetts, 1991.

Kierkegaard, Soren, *Fear and Trembling,* A & D Publishing, Radford, Virginia, Wilder Publications, 2008.

Kierkegaard, Soren, Moore, Charles E., ed., *Provocations, Spiritual Writings of Kierkegaard,* Orbis Books, Maryknoll, New York, 2007.

Lamsa, George M., *Idioms In the Bible Explained and A Key to the Original Gospels,* Harper and Row, Publishers, San Francisco, 1985.

Lewis, C. S., *The Great Divorce,* The Macmillan Company, New York, New York, Fifteenth Printing, 1966.

Little, Paul, *Know What and Why You Believe Two Christian Classics in One Volume,* World Wide Publications, Special Crusade Edition printed for the Billy Graham Evangelistic Association; Minneapolis, Minnesota, 1980.

Maier, Christl M., *Daughter Zion, Mother Zion,* Fortress Press, Minneapolis, Minnesota, 2008.

McCartney, Bill and Lindi, *Sold Out Becoming Man Enough To Make A Difference,* Word Publishing, Nashville, Tennessee, 1997.

McDowell, Josh, *The New Evidence That Demands A Verdict,* Thomas Nelson Publishers, Nashville, Tennessee, 1999.

O'Brien, Julia M., *Challenging Prophetic Metaphor: Theology and Ideology in the Prophets,* Westminster John Knox Press, Louisville, Kentucky, 2008.

Ortlund, Raymond C., Jr., *God's Unfaithful Wife,* InterVarsity Press, Downers Grove, Illinois, 1996.

Pinson, William M., Jr., *Baptists and Religious Liberty,* Baptist Way Press, Dallas, Texas, 2007.

Ramm, Bernard, *Protestant Biblical Interpretation A Textbook of Hermeneutics,* Third Revised Edition, Baker Book House, Grand Rapids, Michigan, sixth printing 1974.

Ryken, Leland; Wilhoit, James C.; Longman, Tremper, III; editors, *Dictionary of Biblical Imagery,* InterVarsity Press, Downers

Grove, Illinois, 1998.

Shelly, Rubel, *Divorce & Remarriage A Redemptive Theology*, Leafwood Publishers, Abilene, Texas, 2007.

Stiver, Dan R., *The Philosophy of Religious Language Sign, Symbol, and Story*, Blackwell Publishers, Oxford, United Kingdom, 1996.

Thomas, Gary L., *Sacred Marriage*, Zondervan, Grand Rapids, Michigan, 2000.

U. S. *Constitution*, Amendment I.

Vaught, Carl G., *Metaphor, Analogy, and the Place of Places Where Religion and Philosophy Meet*, Baylor University Press, Waco, Texas, 2004.

Walvoord, John F., *Every Prophecy of the Bible*, Chariot Victor Publishing, Colorado Springs, Colorado, 1999.

White, Thomas, "Adoption The Heart of the Gospel," *Southwestern News*, Southwestern Baptist Theological Seminary Communications Group, Forth Worth, Texas, Winter 2009, Volume 67, No. 2.